THE PRINCIPAL AS

Leader of the
Equitable
School

INTRODUCTION TO THE
LEADING STUDENT ACHIEVEMENT SERIES

The *Leading Student Achievement* series is a joint publication of the Ontario Principals' Council (OPC) and Corwin Press as part of an active commitment to support and develop excellent school leadership. One of the roles of OPC is to identify, design, develop, and deliver workshops that meet the learning needs of school leaders. Most of the handbooks in this series were originally developed as one-day workshops by their authors to share their expertise in key areas of school leadership. The seven handbooks in this series are these:

- *The Principal as Leader of the Equitable School*
- *The Principal as Leader of Challenging Conversations*
- *The Principal as Professional Learning Community Leader*
- *The Principal as Data-Driven Leader*
- *The Principal as Early Literacy Leader*
- *The Principal as Instructional Leader in Literacy*
- *The Principal as Mathematics Leader*

Each handbook in the *Leading Student Achievement* series is grounded in action and is designed as a hands-on, practical guide to support school leaders in their roles as instructional leaders. From novice principals who are assuming the principalship to experienced principals who are committed to continuous learning, readers from all levels of experience will benefit from the accessible blend of theory and practice presented in these handbooks. The provision of practical strategies that principals can use immediately in their schools makes this series a valuable resource to all who are committed to improving student achievement.

THE PRINCIPAL AS

Leader of the Equitable School

LEADING STUDENT ACHIEVEMENT
SERIES

A Joint Publication

CORWIN
A SAGE Company

FOR INFORMATION:

Corwin
A SAGE Company
2455 Teller Road
Thousand Oaks, California 91320
(800) 233-9936
www.corwin.com

SAGE Publications Ltd.
1 Oliver's Yard
55 City Road
London EC1Y 1SP
United Kingdom

SAGE Publications India Pvt. Ltd.
B 1/I 1 Mohan Cooperative Industrial Area
Mathura Road, New Delhi 110 044
India

SAGE Publications Asia-Pacific Pte. Ltd.
3 Church Street
#10-04 Samsung Hub
Singapore 049483

Printed in the United States of America

Library of Congress Cataloging-in-Publication Data

The principal as leader of the equitable school / Ontario Principals' Council.

p. cm.—(Leading student achievement series)

"A joint publication with Ontario Principals' Council."

Includes bibliographical references and index.

ISBN 978-1-4129-8117-0 (pbk.)

1. School principals—Professional relationships—Ontario. 2. Educational leadership—Ontario. 3. Multicultural education—Ontario. 4. Inclusive education—Ontario. I. Ontario Principals' Council.

LB2831.926.C2P75 2012
371.2′01209713—dc23   2012009213

This book is printed on acid-free paper.

Acquisitions Editor: Debra Stollenwerk
Associate Editor: Desirée A. Bartlett
Editorial Assistant: Kimberly Greenberg
Production Editor: Cassandra Margaret Seibel
Copy Editor: Cate Huisman
Typesetter: C&M Digitals (P) Ltd.
Proofreader: Susan Schon
Indexer: Jean Casalegno
Cover Designer: Scott Van Atta
Permissions Editor: Adele Hutchinson

MIX
Paper from responsible sources
FSC
www.fsc.org
FSC® C014174

17 18 10 9 8 7 6 5 4 3

Contents

Preface

The Principal as Leader of the Equitable School is designed to assist principals and all school leaders in expanding awareness of equity issues, nurturing a spirit of activism in addressing these issues, and developing ideas and strategies for working with others toward those ends. It is based on the premise that awareness and celebration of diversity, although important, are not sufficient to ensure that all students are well served and have equitable chances to learn and achieve. Acknowledging the complexity associated with this topic, this book presents a blend of theory and practice and provides concrete strategies for continuing the journey toward more equitable schools.

Much of the book's content stems from the work of the OPC Equity and Inclusive Education Team. For several years, this team has been designing and implementing workshops, web modules, and conferences to assist principals in addressing issues of equity and inclusive education in their schools and school communities. It is the authors' position that this book will provide an overarching framework for considering the approaches to leading student achievement presented in the other books within the series.

Rationale: Schools in the 21st century are complex sites. On one hand, growing diversity provides exciting opportunities for everyone to be enriched by the experiences, customs, skills, and worldviews of diverse student and community populations. On the other hand, the challenges of ensuring that everyone in this evolving context has the respect, voice, power, and support necessary for a rich and relevant education are real and pressing. Because schools reflect the society around them, students and families who are not a part of the dominant culture still face substantial barriers in meeting with success.

The Principal as Leader of the Equitable School acknowledges the centrality of the principal's role as a catalyst and a perpetuator of change toward more inclusive and equitable school environments. It is designed to provide school leaders with the tools requisite to engage meaningfully and strategically in this process.

The book is grounded in a number of underlying assumptions that include the following:

- Racism, religious intolerance, homophobia, and gender-based violence are still evident in our communities and—unfortunately—in our schools. "These and other discriminatory beliefs and actions should not be seen as forces to which schools must adjust or for which schools must compensate; rather schools should be leading the way and allowing society to respond to innovations in schooling and education" (Delhi, 1995, p. 21).
- "The significant new investments in education are not reaching many of the children who need the most help because long-identified barriers to learning are not being addressed." (McMurtry & Curling, 2008, p. 3).
- "Inclusion is not bringing people into what already exists; it is making a new space, a better space for everyone" (Dei, 2006).
- Students who feel welcomed and respected, accepted, and celebrated in their schools are more likely to meet with academic success, to reach their highest potential, to improve their life chances, and to contribute to a more inclusive and democratic society. There is an increasing body of research showing that students who feel connected to school—to teachers, to other students, and to the school itself—do better academically (Blum, McNeely, & Rinehart, 2002; Schargel, Thacker, & Bell, 2007).
- In a truly equitable system, factors such as race, gender, and socioeconomic status do not prevent students from achieving ambitious outcomes. Our experience shows that barriers can be removed when all education partners create the conditions needed for success (Ontario Ministry of Education, 2008).

This book is designed to meet the challenges of this sociocultural context and to contribute to its improvement.

Audience: No matter where principals are on the continuum of understanding and actively engaging in creating more equitable schools, this book should be of use. Foundational information and activities for heightening personal awareness of equity issues will assist those who are in the early stages of considering how our schools would better serve the students and families who have been traditionally marginalized. For those well on the way in strategically addressing these needs, the reflections, case studies, and activities will provide ideas for working with staff, students, and community to further the work of actively confronting inequitable practices and removing barriers for students who have been underserved. This book would also be a valuable handbook for school equity committees, principal preparation courses, and professional development sessions on improving equity and inclusive education.

APPROACH AND ORGANIZATION

Although the book grounds its practical suggestions clearly in relevant theory, its main thrust is to provide concrete strategies and applications. For this purpose, it is presented as a handbook, divided into eight chapters.

Chapter 1 addresses the essential question: *Why is leading for equity and diversity important?* Drawing upon current demographic and contextual (local, national, and global) information as well as a brief selection of relevant research, this chapter takes a look at the current education environment and the challenges that we as school leaders face in ensuring that equity is at the forefront of what we do to ensure optimal learning for all of our students.

Chapter 2 looks at some of the understandings that are foundational for leading equitable schools. Definitions are provided. A brief overview is provided of the purposes of education; accountability issues and the concepts of power and privilege and their centrality to removing barriers are addressed. Characteristics of leadership that promote inclusive education and serve traditionally marginalized students are outlined.

Chapter 3 focuses on the self and the inner work necessary to move forward on the personal journey to being more equitable and inclusive in our work. This chapter extends an invitation to

- *unearth,*
- *unravel,* and
- *understand* personal stories of individual/group and systemic oppression and, as a result of this process, to
- *unfold* reconsidered attitudes and responses.

Chapter 4 turns to strategies for collaboratively creating a school climate that promotes equity. Central to this chapter is the onus on school leaders to develop an equitable environment and strategies for working with others to ensure that this is a priority. Community partnerships and student outcomes are presented as pivotal issues.

Chapter 5 explores approaches to working specifically with school staff, including teachers, caretakers, secretaries, educational assistants, and all others who work as part of the school team. It addresses the difficult but necessary work of engaging staff in conversations that have traditionally been avoided in school meetings. It also suggests strategies for addressing oppressive acts and embracing a culturally relevant pedagogy.

Chapter 6 focuses on working with students to foster greater equity and inclusive education. Central to this chapter are the questions: "How do school leaders provide space for all students to flourish in equitable ways?" and "How do we elicit students' voices and involve them in working toward socially just ends?" Inclusive curricula using the James Banks (Toronto District School Board, n.d.) and "windows and mirrors" (Style, 1996) models are discussed. In addition, this chapter looks at fostering student leadership and voice, including suggestions for student action research. It considers the importance of formally honoring the diverse student skills and contributions that are not considered to be part of the formal curriculum and assessment processes.

Chapter 7 addresses strategies for building partnerships with school communities to enhance inclusion and to engage families in creating a vision for an equitable school. Approaches are suggested for getting to know your community, enhancing capacity for working toward inclusive education, and building communication bridges.

Finally, *Chapter 8* presents a detailed and specific tool, the *Equity Walk,* that may be used to assess progress within your school. This tool will be useful for establishing a "current state of affairs," identifying gaps and setting specific goals for moving your school along on the journey toward recognizing oppressive practices and working toward a more equitable and antioppressive school environment. As such, it can become an integral part of both formal and informal school improvement planning.

SPECIAL FEATURES

This book provides a variety of practical special features to assist school leaders in their quest to create more equitable schools.

Reflection Activity: In order to consolidate and expand the content of each chapter, a reflection activity is provided for personal and/or collaborative work.

Case Studies: Following each chapter, a case study is provided for personal reflection and/or for use as a professional development tool in working with staff. Each case study is followed by suggested questions for probing the issues raised.

Principals' Action Steps: Each chapter culminates with three short, specific action steps, described as *Self, Others,* and *Try Tomorrow.*

- In the *Self* section, leaders are asked to reflect upon a specific aspect of the chapter contents.
- In the *Others* section, links are provided to short web modules that will be useful in extending discussion and providing ideas associated with the contents of each chapter. These modules are rich sources of insight by recognized leaders in the field of equity. They also provide opportunities to see what equity work looks like in the context of real schools. Reflective questions accompany each of these modules.
- *Try Tomorrow* suggests a specific "to do" item for implementing a concrete, specific strategy.

Tools and Resources: A separate section at the back of the book provides easy access to tools, templates, and activities that have been referred to throughout the chapters. The comprehensive *Equity Walk Template* is also included in this section.

The Three Main Reasons to Purchase This Book

Grounded in relevant theory, this book is a *highly accessible, user friendly,* and *practical* source for developing and extending initiatives in the vitally important process of making our schools more welcoming, inclusive, and equitable places.

Acknowledgments

The Ontario Principals' Council gratefully acknowledges Lynette Spence, Coleen Stewart, and Poleen Grewal, the coauthors of *The Principal as Leader of the Equitable School.*

Lynette Spence is presently employed at the University of Toronto at Hart House in the role of coordinator of equity and diversity initiatives. She was born in Guyana and came to Toronto via Jamaica and London, England. She has held a variety of roles within the school system, including coordinator of antiracism and ethnocultural equity. She retired, as a principal, from the Toronto District School Board. Lynette's passion for equity has led her to develop and deliver workshops on equity and inclusive education all over Ontario. Her involvement with the Ontario Principals' Council began with teaching in the Principals' Qualification Program and has extended to coordinating projects and working with OPC Protective Services consultants in mediating disputes involving OPC members. Commencing in July 2008, Lynette was contracted by OPC to coordinate the Equity and Inclusion Project. (In 2009 and 2010, this project also received funding from the Ontario Ministry of Education.)

Coleen Stewart currently teaches graduate courses in the Theory and Policy in Education Department at the Ontario Institute for Studies in Education / University of Toronto (OISE/UT). She completed her PhD at the same university, with a focus on leadership for diversity and social justice. Her professional background includes a variety of teaching, resource, and administrative roles, including principalships of several elementary schools. Her involvement with OPC includes contributing to the development of equity and inclusive education workshops and web modules for school leaders.

Poleen Grewal is currently employed by the Peel District School Board in a coordinating principal role, school effectiveness leader. In this role, Poleen has ensured that culturally responsive practices are seen as an important part of the teaching and learning process. She is also currently pursuing her doctoral degree at OISE/ UT in the area of sociology and equity studies. Her thesis will focus on how system leaders (e.g., superintendents, principals) negotiate spaces for equity/diversity issues in the current student-achievement focused agenda.

The Ontario Principals' Council also wishes to gratefully acknowledge the contributions of the Equity and Inclusive Education Team: Lynette Spence, Joy Reiter, Joe Santalucia, and Coleen Stewart. In addition, the efforts of Linda Massey on the Ontario Principals' Council in coordinating the joint OPC/Corwin project are gratefully acknowledged.

CHAPTER ONE

Why Leading for Equity and Diversity Is Important

Do we know the names, the faces, and the stories of students who are in danger of failure nine months from now? The inevitable answer is that we know . . . therefore, the only relevant question is whether we have the will to apply that knowledge to meet the needs of our students.

(Reeves, 2006)

During the early 1990s, when I was working as an equity coordinator in a large urban school district, I was asked by an elementary school principal to meet with some "Black" students in Grade 8 who felt that their knowledge(s) and experiences were being excluded from the classroom and the school environment. I don't remember all the details of our conversation in that meeting but I will never forget the *cri de coeur* coming from one of the girls, Stephanie: "I'm just tired, tired of Columbus. I want to do something else."

As the conversation continued, it became clear that the reference to Christopher Columbus was not only about the Columbus "myth" itself but also pointed to something larger and more important. The "discovery of America" is, for some students, their first exposure in the history classroom to "the encounter between two cultures, the encounter between two races" (Bigelow & Peterson, 1998). As such, it may be the starting point of an educational journey that clearly

1

demonstrates how the perspectives of people of color have been disregarded in the official curriculum. We know that there can be great danger for children when a single story such as the Columbus "myth" is the beginning of what can be a winners' history that silences the perspectives of people of color and all the "Others." An ancient African proverb expresses it this way: "Until lions have their own historians, tales of the hunt will always glorify the hunter."

Digging more deeply into Stephanie's comment provides school leaders with a host of entry points for rethinking and rearticulating an equity and inclusive education strategy for their educational institutions. For Stephanie and the other Grade 8 girls in that meeting, school was a site for addressing and negotiating identity. However, their narratives portray school as a place where they are denied opportunities to see the world through their eyes and to analyze the causes and effects of power relationships in their immediate environment and in the larger society. Implicit in the students' dialogue also seems to be a longing and desire for the inclusion of pedagogies that incorporate and emphasize their everyday lives and the consideration of race, social class, and gender. Among cultural studies theorists, this question of whose culture is being studied receives pressing attention as does the issue of which instruments should be used to study that culture. As school leaders with a responsibility for ensuring that all students can learn effectively, we must therefore strive to intentionally implement a more representative curriculum, alternative teaching strategies, and positive social relations in our schools. How can we empower groups with the least power to practically develop their own readings of and their own responses to received knowledge in order to articulate their own identities? That is one of our biggest challenges.

CURRENT CONTEXTS

Schooling in the 21st century has become an increasingly complex activity as the entire school community assumes more challenging roles in support of meeting and serving the diverse needs of all learners. In certain urban centers in North America, multiracial, multiethnic, and multicultural diversity is rapidly and increasingly becoming the norm due to immigration and birth patterns. To quote one of my colleagues, "We are now the caretakers of the world's children." According to Lisa Delpit, these are *our* children; they are not "other people's children" (Delpit, 1995).

Going to school remains a key transitional event in all our lives. School is a place where we all come together with our embodiments of race, sex, gender, socioeconomic class, and ability/disability. The opening narrative also demonstrates that school can also be the place where the educational process produces subjects through a variety of discourses, policies, and practices. There is a wealth of well-researched findings that prove that educational institutions are responsible for perpetuating the inequities embedded within North American society. Researchers such as Brookover and Lezotte (1979) and Lezotte (1997) provide evidence that learning and achievement among students from similar backgrounds varies significantly based on the practices of their schools. Some of the research also shows that the formal education system has not been, for the most part, accepting of alternatives that have not conformed to neoliberal principles and beliefs. In other words, educational policy reform in North America has been predominantly influenced by economic theory, with its discourse of market methods, efficiency, productivity, and rankings.

Equity-seeking groups and individuals, however, argue that inequality, poverty, racism, sexism, homophobia, and other discriminatory beliefs and actions should not be seen as forces to which schools must adjust or for which schools must compensate; rather, schools should be leading the way in ensuring that all students, with all their embodiments, learn effectively. In this way, schools provide a model that compels society to respond to innovations in schooling and education. The Ontario Ministry of Education (2008) supports this view in its affirmation that "in a truly equitable system, factors such as race, gender, and socioeconomic status do not prevent students from achieving ambitious outcomes. Our experience shows that barriers can be removed when all education partners create the conditions needed for success" (p. 8). Herein perhaps lies the makings of a new role for public education. Instead of restructuring schools to match a changing society, schools will change the societal paradigm by restructuring society instead of reacting to society.

I invite you to return to a time not so long ago when schools became the leaders in raising awareness about homophobia and in encouraging the entire school community to respond to the needs of lesbian, gay, bisexual, transgender, and queer (LGBTQ) students. Although tensions continue to surface for these communities in North America, the establishment of Gay-Straight Alliance groups was a huge step in creating safe spaces for LGBTQ students. These groups are now actively working in schools to support immediate intervention on issues related to sexual orientation and gender equity. Policy development and implementation and formal discourse on particular LGBTQ issues have produced a change in school climate by making strategic recommendations for addressing heterosexist and homophobic attitudes, behaviors, and practices.

Such a process requires that educators move beyond mere discussions that hint at educational reform to address genuine, fundamental, systemic transformation. For example, when I was a secondary school vice principal, I noticed that one of our senior students was absent from school for long periods of time. After a conversation with his parents, who mentioned that there was a problem that was being addressed by their pastor, I had a meeting with the student. His disclosure that he was gay and being harassed at school set off a series of conversations among administrators, staff, students, and parents about schoolwide support for gay students. We initiated and developed a school policy and plan with action steps, timelines, responsibilities, et cetera around an education process on LGBTQ issues for the entire school community. I remember receiving a number of positive letters from both straight and gay students, as well as their parents, congratulating our school on its efforts toward systemic change.

The insertion/addition of African Studies courses into the secondary school history curriculum, the current international languages curriculum, and the development of the Ontario First Nation, Métis and Inuit Education Policy Framework are excellent examples of policymakers and school leaders leading the way in transforming schools and society. In some school districts, courses in First Nations and Pacific Rim languages, for example, are available for all students as are other heritage languages.

Lindsey, Roberts, and CampbellJones (2005) in their book *The Culturally Proficient School: An Implementation Guide for School Leaders* tell the story of a school whose data analysis revealed that many recent immigrant students of Mexican ancestry were absent from school for long periods around the times of cultural events such as Christmas and Easter when they returned to visit relatives in the home country. As a result, these students missed as much as three weeks of classroom work that left them far behind other students. Consultations and conferencing with parents were unsuccessful in shifting the strong cultural pull of family celebrations. In looking for solutions to the situation, the school leadership team realized that the current school organization was serving the types of families who had long migrated from the area. The team proposed that the school calendar be organized to fit the lifestyle patterns of the current cohort of families. The school then instituted a calendar with a winter break for four weeks in late December and early January and for two weeks during the observance of Passion and Easter weeks.

One of my colleagues recounts a similar shift that took place in a First Nations community in the Canadian North, where the school calendar was adjusted to acknowledge and honor families who needed to be together during the fishing, hunting, and trapping seasons.

Leading for equity and diversity must therefore be motivated by an urgent need to address what has to change in order to ensure successful outcomes for each and every learner. We all know that it is no easy task to create and sustain broad system change. In the case of transforming schools to institutions that will lead the way for society to follow, it will become the responsibility of the principal and the entire school community to redefine the central concepts of formal education and more specifically to develop and deliver priorities and processes to meet the needs of all students and their families. In a 2008 Equity and Inclusive Education Symposium on Human Rights, Antiracism, and Cultural Proficiency hosted by the Ontario Principals' Council, one of the panelists made the following assertion:

I do though want to push us on challenging ourselves. I think we have to get down to the very grassroots about ourselves before we can really be comfortable enough to deal with things in the way we want to in our schools, and unless we are really internally comfortable with the conversation as leaders, we're not going to be able to help all the folks on either end of that continuum understand and bring them together. (Worthy, 2008)

A very long time ago, the late Ron Edmonds, one of the founders of the Effective Schools Movement, put it this way:

We can, whenever and wherever we choose, successfully teach all students whose schooling is of interest to us. We already know more than we need in order to do that. Whether we do it or not will finally depend on how we feel about the fact that we haven't so far. (1979, p. 23)

These three declarative sentences carry as much weight today. Dr. Larry Lezotte, one of Ron Edmonds' colleagues and one of the original members of the Effective Schools Movement, makes an additional declaration: "It is time for compulsory schooling to be transformed into compulsory learning." This simple shift—from a focus on teaching to a focus on learning—has profound implications for schools.

It seems appropriate at this time to draw a distinction between student learning and student achievement. Mark Twain once said, "I have never let my schooling interfere with my education." Education is not preparing students for a world that is fixed and static. The postmodern world is defined and marked by difference, discontinuity, and disruption. Knowing and understanding that this is so compels us to rethink received knowledge, official stories, cultural representations, and current pedagogies inside of schooling. Many definitions of success and achievement are bound up with all kinds of normative assumptions that place restrictions on students' learning. It is common knowledge that standardized testing data are being used as catalysts to drive dialogue on student learning and academic improvement. Instead of being data driven, school leaders should strive to become data informed. Instead of focusing on the children's deficits, data collection, analysis, and reporting should focus on deficits in the curriculum and the environment that do not facilitate learning for all. Currently these conversations seem to disregard the biases in the assessment processes and focus on "what the student knows" rather than "how the student comes to know." In my view, learning is about the latter, and currently much of it occurs after formal schooling. Leaders of equitable schools must therefore ensure that students view themselves as lifelong learners in the process of learning and that students willingly engage in learning by raising questions, proposing explanations, planning and carrying out activities, communicating in a variety of ways, and critiquing and reflecting on their learning.

THE MORAL IMPERATIVE

The statements from Edmonds and Lezotte compel us to ask critical questions and to incorporate fresh perspectives and mental models into school improvement process models. However, as the panelist from the 2008 Equity and Inclusive Education Symposium reminded us, we must first (re)engage with the moral imperative that is at the center of issues of equity, diversity, and social justice. What do I believe? What do I really value? What are schools for? What is success at school and what does it look like? What is excellence? Is it accessible and also equitable? The Reflection Activity at the end of this chapter is a useful tool for assessing your assumptions, attitudes, dispositions, and behaviors.

It may be a cliché that parents send us the best kids that they've got, but it is one of the entry points as well as a source of intentionality for our work. DuFour, DuFour, Eaker, and Karhanek (2004) remind us that "we should indeed promote high levels of learning for every child entrusted to us, not because of legislation or fear of sanctions, but because we have a moral and ethical imperative to do so" (p. 27). Intentionality about school improvement, increased student achievement, and closing the achievement gap highlights the need to interrupt some of the underlying discourses that occur within the system in the form of teachers' beliefs about children's deficiencies. The thoughts and actions that stem from these beliefs then shape system and school practice, and "blind prospective change agents to students' strengths, and delimit the transformative potential of social justice praxis within urban environments" (Armstrong & McMahon, 2006, p. x).

How many times have you heard statements like these?

- If we didn't have to count the aboriginal students or the Hispanic students or . . . , our scores would be higher.
- We never get any support from the parents; they never show up for interviews; they never return our calls.
- All kids used to come to kindergarten with oral language; now most of them come with no oral language.
- They should be in the applied level stream, not advanced.
- I only work with the best and the brightest. I have no time for the others.

It's always about the kids or the parents, and it's always a focus on "them" and not on "us" and our practices. The story told earlier about the school that changed its curriculum calendar to bring it into alignment with the living patterns of its students and families is an excellent exemplar of shifting leadership standards, attitudes, and behaviors to ensure access to learning for all.

What if we were to think of our students as underserved rather than underperforming? This notion is at the center of the Cultural Proficiency Continuum (Lindsey, Roberts, & CampbellJones, 2005). There are six points along the Cultural Proficiency Continuum (Figure 1.1) that indicate unique ways of perceiving and responding to difference. During their highly recommended Annual Cultural Proficiency Institute, Lindsey, Nuri Robins, and Terrell delve into the capsule annotations that describe each point on the continuum as well as provide examples to expand the understanding of each concept.

The first three locations on the left side of the continuum—*cultural destructiveness, cultural incapacity,* and *cultural blindness*—demonstrate individuals' and organizations' limited tolerance for diversity. The other three locations on the right side of the continuum—*cultural precompetence, cultural competence,* and *cultural proficiency*—highlight the transformation for equity. Stephanie Graham, Los Angeles County Office of Education, has adapted the Cultural Proficiency Continuum by developing a

Figure 1.1   Cultural Proficiency Continuum

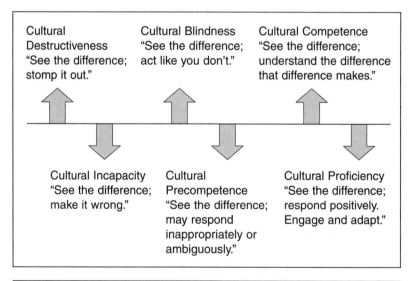

Cultural Destructiveness
"See the difference; stomp it out."

Cultural Blindness
"See the difference; act like you don't."

Cultural Competence
"See the difference; understand the difference that difference makes."

Cultural Incapacity
"See the difference; make it wrong."

Cultural Precompetence
"See the difference; may respond inappropriately or ambiguously."

Cultural Proficiency
"See the difference; respond positively. Engage and adapt."

Source: From *Cultural Proficiency: A Manual for School Leaders,* 2nd ed, by R. B. Lindsey, K. Nuri Robins, and R. D. Terrell, 2003, Thousand Oaks, CA: Corwin. Reprinted with permission.

template that describes historical and current situations and contexts, individual behaviors, and policies and practices of organizations that fall within each point on the continuum. Her template, entitled "Six Levels of Workplace Cultural Proficiency (Workplace and School Settings)," may be found in the Tools and Resources Section at the end of this book.

Both individually and organizationally, the journey along the continuum toward cultural proficiency will be a long, difficult one, strewn with bumps and bruises. We would need to shift from a risk-based, deficit model of diversity in all its dimensions as illustrated in the negative assessments of students' abilities mentioned earlier to an assets- or strengths-based understanding of diversity. Lindsey et al. (2005) provide a visual matrix to delineate the shift, as shown in Figure 1.2.

This would also result in moving school leaders beyond sameness to recognize that our students are not a monolithic group and that we must honor the multiple identities that they bring with them into educational spaces. Here is one school's example of honoring

Figure 1.2   Changing Paradigms

Cultural proficiency helps us to move . . .	
. . . from tolerance for diversity . . . *Destructiveness—Blindness*	*. . . to transformation for equity.* *Precompetence—Proficiency*
Focus on "them" and their inadequacies	Focus on "us" and our practices
Demographics viewed as challenge	Demographics inform policy and practice
Prevent, mitigate, avoid cultural dissonance and conflict	Manage, leverage, facilitate conflict
Stakeholders expect or help others to assimilate	Stakeholders adapt to meet needs of others
Information added to existing policies, procedures, practices	Information integrated into policies, procedures, practices

Source: Lindsey, Roberts, and CampbellJones (2005).

the identities of its students and community: For the past three years, Valley Park Middle School has permitted the local Muslim community to offer a Friday afternoon prayer in the school cafeteria for part of the year. Students need parental permission letter to attend. There have been no problems or complaints to date. This creative solution came out of teachers' concerns that as many as 400 students were missing classes when they attended prayers at the closest mosque. In fact, many students never returned to school after Friday prayers. Now a national advocacy group has launched a campaign to repeal what they describe as "brazen attempts to Islamize the school district." In Valley Park's view, however, the school feels that it is putting the needs of the students first and using demographics to inform policy and practice.

KNOWLEDGE, DIFFERENCE, AND DIVERSITY

All partners in education must therefore continue to advocate, lead, and keep at the center of their practice and visions, the issues of race, class, gender, disability, sexual orientation, and other historical forms of marginalization. Education remains a site of contestation, where the competing voices of all the partners in a complex, political arena reverberate to make sure that the fundamental educational question of "What knowledge is of most worth?" is transformed—as it should be—into the even more challenging question of "Whose knowledge is of most worth?" Questions such as these, and other questions such as, "What constitutes 'knowledge'?" and "Whose 'knowledge' is being taught?" have been objects of enquiry for educators for decades. This is the place from which Stephanie cried out.

   We have come to understand from sociologists that how a society selects, classifies, distributes, transmits, and evaluates public official knowledge reflects both the distribution of power and the principles of social control. Sociologists also tell us that education is a selection and organization from all the available knowledge(s) at a particular time, which involves conscious and unconscious choices. These views, which speak to the fact that knowledge is socially organized and constructed, mandate that matters of intellectual content and organization in schooling receive serious attention from school leaders in creating equitable schools.

Some current approaches in rethinking issues of race, identity, ethnicity, and culture suggest that educators must begin to examine them in global and relational terms despite the specific contextual locations in which schools operate. We are all familiar with the term *global village* and are becoming familiar with the term *global media.* People read about, hear about, and react to global news instantly. School knowledge is not isolated from what is happening in the world outside the school door. An exploration and analysis of the relationships among different social groups in Canada and the United States, and the relationship between developments in the United States and Canada and developments in the rest of the world, merits a central place in the official school curriculum. For example, what are the links between "Western" industrial development and the underdevelopment and exploitation of Third World countries? I remember Cameron McCarthy in a lecture asking individuals to consider the far-reaching effects of the civil rights movement in the United States on the expansion of democratic practices to excluded groups in Australia, the Caribbean, Africa, and even the United States itself. If not today, one day very soon, our students will certainly be studying the multiplier effects of the 2011 Arab Spring on the emergence of other world voices yearning for change.

It is by emphasizing this "relationality of knowledge," to use Cameron McCarthy's phrase (McCarthy, 1993) that we might finally be able to explore the question of what constitutes "knowledge" and its corollaries. George Dei (2003) insists that "no one must be left outside the school door." This places a huge obligation on teachers to ensure that they teach to their students' knowledges, that they do not simply avoid problems by creating artificial boundaries between schools and communities, and that they do not pathologize minoritized communities in accounting for student failures while schools take credit for students' successes. We continue to hear teachers lament the fact that kindergarten students used to arrive at school with no need to even prime the pump to turn on their learning power, and now "these kids" don't even come with any oral language. During the Symposium referenced earlier, one of the speakers noted that such a statement was an example of systemic oppression, since "these kids" did have oral language—the language of the home. It may not be the language of the school, but it is oral language.

Placing emphasis on both the diversity and relationality of knowledge opens up spaces for learners to cease being passive consumers of "official" stories and become active participants in producing their own representations, narrating their own stories, and engaging in dialogue and collaborative investigation. I remember a visit to a Grade 11 history class where students were studying a chapter on Islam from an approved textbook. One of the students rose to state that she was offended by the author's portrayal of certain aspects of the religion—her religion, her way of life. She then presented certain additional perspectives and offered to rewrite the chapter for her classmates and for future students' use.

The following poem, written by students Fan Wu and Oyeyinka Oyelowo within an extracurricular club (Students Working Against Great Injustice [SWAG]), is an illustration of student storytelling.

Our community is so divided and brittle,

Governments do nothing but degrade and belittle.

Our capacity and potential are never considered,

Fear and prejudice keep us caged and injured.

We must change our perception of the unknown,

Our egos cannot sit on some untouchable throne.

Our hate is not just words, but knives,

*Slaughtering our children and beating our wives.

Emancipate yourself from the leash society places,

Love each other no matter the colour of our faces.

*This line is excluded from use with elementary school students.

FRAMEWORKS FOR ACTION

In the last three decades, a rich body of research literature has been developed for both theoretical and practical models that have moved equity and inclusive education beyond theory to action- and activist-oriented approaches and strategies that are creating schools where all students can learn effectively.

In the ensuing chapters, we will further demonstrate the strength of models such as the Cultural Proficiency Framework.

Cultural proficiency is the policies and practices of an organization or the values and behaviors of an individual that enable the agency or person to interact effectively in a culturally diverse environment. Cultural proficiency is reflected in the way an organization treats its employees, its clients, and its community. (Lindsey et al., 1999, p. 21)

Another model we present is the James Banks framework, which comprises five dimensions—content integration, knowledge construction, prejudice reduction, equity pedagogy, and empowering school culture—as well as four stages or levels—the Contributions Approach, the Additive Approach, the Transformation Approach, and the Social Action Approach. Both models are most useful for maintaining a practical and critical gaze on our work.

One of the entry points for doing work in equity and inclusive education is one's own personal experiences; this entry point is the foundation of Chapter 3. However, working with allies and building coalitions are essential, both philosophically and practically. Recent policy documents from the Ontario Ministry of Education— *Realizing the Promise of Diversity: Ontario's Equity and Inclusive Education Strategy* (2009b), and *Equity and Inclusive Education in Ontario Schools: Guidelines for Policy Development and Implementation* (2009a)—which identify eight areas of focus and illustrate their key connections and relevance to other ministry programs and initiatives, are high-quality foundational pieces in this area. The focus areas[1] are the following:

1. Board policies, programs, guidelines, and practices

2. Shared and committed leadership

3. School–community relationships

4. Inclusive curriculum and assessment practices

5. Religious accommodation

6. School climate and the prevention of discrimination and harassment

7. Professional learning

8. Accountability and transparency

These tools and frameworks are key pillars and supports in the effort to take the politics of difference and diversity seriously and to redefine, reframe, and respond to the full range of needs within the education community.

Chapter Summary

Schools begin to change only when leaders use equity as a lens through which they recognize the disparities that exist between students who are well served in the system and those who are underserved. Equity is not about treating everyone the same. Students, families, and communities are not a monolithic group, and we must advocate, lead, and keep at the center of our practice and visions the issues of race, class, gender, disability, sexual orientation, and other historical forms of marginalization. Many of us have been "normalized" to seeing and being in the world in particular ways depending upon our cultural and life experiences. On the whole, schools in North America still tend to be dominated by a professional, White, middle class culture. In the next chapter, we examine the need to unpack our assumptions about ourselves and others. This is a highly personal and sometimes difficult process, but we must engage in it if we are going to be able to relate in meaningful ways to all members of our school community. There is a vast continuum of progress on that journey. We need to honor and respect where people are, and create safe spaces for nudging each other along.

Case Study: Negotiating Barriers to Student Success

Michael is the only son of a single mother and is enrolled in Grade 2 at Happy Valley Public School. His mother was educated in a district that she believes systemically stereotyped and discriminated against her. She is bright and capable and has overcome many obstacles to become successful in her own life. She has achieved this in spite of being directed into inappropriate programs with low expectations throughout her school career.

As principal of Happy Valley PS, you have received reports that her son has become increasingly problematic and difficult to manage. He has difficulty paying attention and has exhibited increasing acts of spontaneous physical aggression toward staff and other students. When this case is brought to the school team, the strong recommendation is for testing and support for the child. However, every time you contact the mother, she flatly refuses support, refuses to have her son tested, and dismisses the school's concerns as discriminatory, exaggerated, or too trivial. She points to both her own experience and current literature to state that any consequence the school imposes on her child for his behavior will be an act of racism. Meanwhile, Michael continues to be challenged both academically and socially in his day-to-day behaviors, and other parents and staff are pressing you to act.

1. Describe your interior monologue as you prepare for a conversation with Michael's mother. Consider the codes and patterns that govern you in your relationships with parents and students.

2. How do you acknowledge the mother's lived experiences shaped along racial lines?

3. What would the conversation sound like?

4. What are the equity issues that are presented in this case study?

REFLECTION ACTIVITY

Reflection Statement	YES—In our school, I/we demonstrate this in the following ways:	NO—In our school, I/we will initiate this in the following ways:
1. I believe that each and every student can learn.	✓	
2. I understand that equity is not treating everyone the same.	✓	
3. I have high expectations for all learners.	✓+	

(Continued)

(Continued)

Reflection Statement	YES—In our school, I/we demonstrate this in the following ways:	NO—In our school, I/we will initiate this in the following ways:
4. I focus on the learner, and the learner is at the center of all teaching and learning in our school.		✓
5. I model respectful behavior and expect responsible behavior from all learners.	✓	
6. I am prepared to advocate for change and to address issues of access and equity for all learners.		✓
7. I am prepared to examine my own response to diversity, my attitude toward race and culture, and the ways in which I exercise my power.	✓	
8. I understand basic equity terminology and concepts and I program to challenge the "isms" in our teaching.	✓	
9. I challenge statements and practices of colleagues, parents, and students that are biased.		✓
10. I am open to serving the needs of internationally educated students and parents.	✓	
11. I engage our students in reflecting on their own lives and how they have come to believe and feel as they do.	✓	
12. I feel comfortable in dealing with issues of controversy and tensions around new and differing perspectives in our classrooms and school.	✓	
13. I often operate outside my comfort zone and find it easy to do so.		✓

Reflection Statement	YES—In our school, I/we demonstrate this in the following ways:	NO—In our school, I/we will initiate this in the following ways:
14. I create and use primary source documents/stories that surface and reveal the presence of issues of race, gender, bias, equity, et cetera.		
15. I ask difficult questions about how we are progressing with equity, diversity, and social justice in our school.		
16. I build on what I know about where people are along the continuum of equity and inclusivity.		
17. I do personal, self-reflective, autobiographical study that helps me know what to do with the challenges I face in social justice work.		
18. I share and celebrate my challenges and successes with my colleagues, parents, and students.		
19. I think about, design interventions for, and ask specially focused questions about students not previously well served in our school.		
20. I can guarantee to my colleagues, parents, and students that I take our duty to accommodate seriously and consciously.		
21. I listen respectfully and hear my colleagues', parents', and students' concerns about equity, and I change my behavior as appropriate to further the work.		
22. I don't cave in to any and all complaints regarding equity, diversity, and social justice when people get mad or disagree with me.		
23. I am fully committed to equity, diversity, and social justice.		

Principals' Action Steps

SELF

Review the responses to the reflective activity. Do a gap analysis to highlight actual state (what is) and desired state (what should be).

OTHERS

View the video *Leading Expert Voices From the Field* (Ontario Principals' Council, 2010) at http://www.principals.ca/Display.aspx?cid=8194&pid=8075 with your administrative team and/or school improvement team and/or staff. Respond as a group to the Reflective Questions accompanying the video.

TRY TOMORROW

Select one gap that needs to be filled, and develop at least one strategy that will begin to fill the gap.

Note

1. © Queen's Printer for Ontario, 2009. Reproduced with permission.

CHAPTER TWO

Leading the Equitable School

Foundational Understandings

Leaders need to appreciate the realities that they are over-riding in the pursuit of those that they seek to inculcate.

(Greenfield & Ribbins, 1993, p. 260)

A s educators and school leaders, we take ourselves with us to work each day. We interact with our students, their families, and each other from a position that is shaped by our cultural experiences and multiple identities. Our effectiveness in meeting the needs of our diverse students will depend upon our willingness to unpack our beliefs and to approach inclusive education with an openness to broadening our worldviews. Foundational to our work as leaders in equitable schools are the following:

- Our beliefs about the purposes of education
- Our awareness and understanding of oppression
- Our awareness and understanding of power and privilege
- Our orientations to systems of accountability
- Our ability to apply a "critical consciousness"
- Our commitment to take action as advocates for the students and families in our school communities

This chapter will look at these foundations for our work in schools and suggest aspects of what equitable and inclusive leadership might look like. This will provide a basis for the practical ideas and strategies that are offered throughout the book.

In the box below, you will find definitions of terms that are central to this discussion.

Definitions

Democratic Education: By "democratic," we mean the deep sense of the word, the "open exchange of social and political ideas in public discourse, including the full inclusion and representation of voices and perspectives historically silenced and/or marginalized" (Portelli, Shields, & Vibert, 2007, p. 56).

Diversity: The presence of a wide range of human qualities and attributes within a group, organization, or society. The dimensions of diversity include, but are not limited to, ancestry, culture, ethnicity, gender, gender identity, language, physical and intellectual ability, race, religion, sex, sexual orientation, and socioeconomic status.

Equity: A condition or state of fair, inclusive, and respectful treatment of all people. Equity does not mean treating people the same without regard for individual differences.

Inclusive Education: Education that is based on the principles of acceptance and inclusion of all students. Students see themselves reflected in their curriculum, their physical surroundings, and the broader environment, in which diversity is honored and all individuals are respected.

Oppression: The systematic exclusion and/or disempowering of others on the basis of, but not limited to, ancestry, culture, ethnicity, gender, gender identity, language, physical and intellectual ability, race, religion, sex, sexual orientation, and socioeconomic status.

Source: Adapted from Ontario's Equity and Inclusive Education Strategy, Ontario Ministry of Education (2009b).

PURPOSES OF EDUCATION

Equity in education and equitable leadership rest upon some underlying assumptions about the purposes of education. While there are many purposes, including the provision of knowledge and skills requisite for the world of work, the nurturing of qualities necessary for full engagement in a democratic society are central to our calling as responsible and equitable educators. These skills include the ability to think critically and to develop a voice for engaging in debate and advocating for the needs of all of society's members. As Tomlinson points out,

> Education must not be solely a preparation for the immediate perceived needs of the economy but must help all young people to explore "the sort of life worth aspiring to" (Pring, 1997). It is a process for enabling students to value themselves and others, to "take control of their own lives and, as active citizens, have regard for their duties and responsibilities, as well as their rights" (Gus, 2009, p. ix). (Tomlinson, 2000, p. 12)

With these purposes in mind, the view of a "successful school" subscribed to in this book is one in which

> the learning community sets students on the path of inquiry and gives them tools of reflection, dialogue, and critique to be successful. . . . A good school is transformative. It is an instrument of meaningful change in the lives of individual students, their families, and the wider society. (Shields, 2005)

EXCLUSION AND OPPRESSION

In order to be equitable and inclusive in our practices, it is important that we first understand and acknowledge the nature and effects of exclusion and oppression. It is helpful to consider the feelings and consequences associated with being "excluded." The reflection offered by Ryan (2006) in the box below provides a good starting point.

What Is Exclusion?

If you have been bullied or ostracized, teased or tormented because you were too fat or too skinny, too studious or too slow, you also know what it's like to be excluded. All of us have felt excluded at some time, and

(Continued)

(Continued)

we know all too well the feelings of embarrassment and humiliation that can result. But for some people, exclusion happens every day, repeatedly and systematically. As well as hurting their feelings, it destroys their opportunities and ruins their lives, especially if they are denied educational opportunities and the basic right to learn.

✳ ✳ ✳

If you are forbidden to speak and learn in your own language, if the content of the curriculum and of standardized tests favours other people's cultures more than yours, if your parents are labeled as lazy because they cannot leave their night jobs to get to meetings at the school, or if teachers have only low expectations for you because you are black or female or poor, then the educational exclusion you experience cuts to the core of your life and your opportunities within it.

Source: Ryan (2006, pp. 1–2).

Oppressive or inequitable treatment, such as racism, sexism, heterosexism, or classism, occurs on two levels, individual and systemic. It is easier for principals and teachers to notice and therefore to act to rectify individual acts of exclusion, such as racist comments or ostracism of students who live in poverty. Systemic oppression, however, is often not so easily noticed and therefore has a stronger tendency to persist. Some examples of systemic oppression will help to illustrate the difference.

Consider the following:

- The position of First Nations students who year after year are expected to participate actively in social studies and history lessons about the "building" of Canada and/or the United States from a Eurocentric perspective
- The feelings of exclusion experienced by students who have same sex parents and who must participate in units of study on "the family" that neglect to recognize and appreciate their family structure
- The position of the bilingual Latino student whose skills in translating and interpreting provide a service to the teacher

and to other students but are not formally recognized, because these skills are not a part of the "official" curriculum and assessment processes (Hamann, 2008)

- The position of Muslim students who find that high-stakes tests are scheduled during Ramadan, a time when they may be fasting during the day
- The position of the expert Black teacher on a predominantly White staff in an urban school whose "voice" is heard and valued by school administrators only when they need support with situations and issues involving "difficult" Black students and families

There are several reasons for the tendency of systemic oppression and exclusion to go unnoticed and to persist:

- Practices that have endured for a long time become part of a traditional repertoire.
- Neglecting to develop a culture of "critical consciousness" in schools means that the effects of these normalized approaches remain invisible.
- Some "voices" have more power than others and are more likely to be heard in discussions about curriculum and practices in schools.
- There is considerable pressure on school leaders to present an image of the school that is harmonious and conflict free. (Solomon, 2002)

And so these sensitive topics fester under a veil of silence. They persist as well because of assumptions and beliefs that are based upon erroneous and/or incomplete knowledge. A good example of this would be the concept of "race" that remains dominant as a discourse, and the persistent tendency for Whiteness to be considered a norm to which others are compared.

We share the view that people of good will, when faced with the realities of these injustices and the ways in which they can be perpetuated in schools, will want to move forward in creating more equitable spaces for students and their families. There are many fundamentally decent people who go about their daily lives unaware that the status quo and daily practices that seem "normal" to them unfairly marginalize and oppress others. However, as Chomsky points out,

If they can be brought to raise questions and apply their decent instincts and basic intelligence, many people quickly escape the confines of the doctrinal system and are willing to do something to help others who are really suffering and oppressed. (as cited in Achbar, 1994, p. 195)

For example, for years teachers taught a very Eurocentric curriculum about the "conquest of the West," or the "Westward movement" in America. It seemed "normal" to do so, as this curriculum had been in place for a very long time. When it was brought to their attention that this unfairly represented the lived experiences of First Nations people, they realized that this was in fact the case and began to look for more inclusive ways to address the teaching of history. Looking at the "stories" that perpetuate in schools and society in this way helps to disrupt the unequal relations of power that too often remain unquestioned.

POWER

Power works in many different ways in schools and in society at large. It is important for school leaders to understand, and to help others understand, how power operates, both overtly and invisibly, and how unequal relations of power maintain a status quo that favors some groups more than others.

Authoritarian power is visible in schools in the form of policies, directives, and hierarchical positions. It is visible when, for example, decisions are made at a staff meeting or a school council meeting. The items that make it onto the agenda are an indication of who has a say in deciding what is important. But there is power at play when items do not surface for attention. For example, silence on issues about equity, whether by intent or by lack of awareness, maintains the power of the traditionally dominating culture. Silence, in other words, is action in favor of the status quo.

Power is also at work in the ideas and practices that have come to appear as "normal" in schools, such as tracking, or prescribed curriculum, or engaging in extensive testing practices to sort students. Through regular practice, these processes become "what's done in schools" rather than being questioned and contested when they result in inequitable outcomes. Also crucial is the issue of who controls the school curriculum; who has the power to decide what knowledge, values, and beliefs will be passed on to the next generation; and how knowledge acquisition will be tested (Tomlinson, 2000). It is important for school leaders to be aware of the ways in which power works, in both obvious and subtle ways, to advantage some groups and not others in their schools.

PRIVILEGE

In order for school leaders to move along the continuum toward becoming leaders committed to equity, inclusion, and success for each and every student, it is important to understand the role that privilege and entitlement play in promoting systems of oppression. According to CampbellJones, CampbellJones, and Lindsey (2010),

> a sense of privilege and entitlement arises from indifference to benefits that accrue solely by one's membership in a gender, race, or other cultural group. This barrier encapsulates the practice of denying one group societal benefits, while awarding those same benefits to others. (p. 20)

They point out that continued achievement gaps among certain demographic groups are "evidence of accrued benefits for some and lack thereof for others, passed from one generation to the next" (p. 21). Portelli et al. (2007) provide examples of this process in action by observing that, commonplace notions such as

> school readiness, early and emergent literacies, meritocracy, background knowledge, and previous experience are all based in unexamined assumptions that universalize white middle class habitus (Connell, 1994; Dei, 2002; Finn, 1999). This habit of thought presents daily challenges for students, community members, and teachers working in diverse and high poverty sites. (p. 38)

In other words, we cannot assume that the "markers of success," such as school readiness, that are based on the skills and knowledge that middle class students arrive with, are appropriate criteria to use with students who come from very different circumstances.

For example, primary teachers often consider familiarity with nursery rhymes and folk tales that are from a Eurocentric heritage to be indicators of success in the early years. This assumption privileges those students who come from Eurocentric households and disadvantages those whose folklore and early oral traditions are quite different but still rich. Portelli et al. (2007) are making the point above that our aim should not be to *assimilate* students into the dominant culture's base of knowledge and skills, but to *enrich* the collective culture by broadening that base in ways that honor the traditions and experiences of the multiple groups that are represented in our schools. The Reflective Activity at the end of this chapter will engage you in exploring this issue as it relates to practices in your school.

Notions of power and privilege are particularly pervasive as they relate to race and racism. Pollock suggests that there are four foundational principles that underpin work in simultaneously promoting "racially equal opportunity and counteracting racism" in our schools and school communities. These involve

- rejecting false notions of human difference,
- acknowledging lived experiences shaped along racial lines,
- learning from diverse forms of knowledge and experiences, and
- challenging systems of racial inequality. (Pollock, 2008, p. xviii)

This process is complex, for as Pollock points out, "Antiracism requires not treating people as racial group members when that is harmful, and recognizing them as racial group members when that helps people to analyze life experiences and equalize opportunity" (p. xxii).

WORKING IN SYSTEMS OF ACCOUNTABILITY

Most principals and teachers are living and working within systems of tight, narrowly defined accountability. The forms of educational accountability that currently prevail in North America and throughout much of the industrialized world are rooted in the neoliberal ideals of competition, standardization, and measurement. Even for educators committed to equitable and antioppressive practices, it can be difficult to maintain a strong focus on these issues in light of the pressure for students to perform on formal tests. In fact, research indicates that when faced with a myriad of priorities, even principals who initially resisted formal accountability systems were eventually "normalized" to give increasing time and attention to preparing students for these tasks (Ladd & Zelli, 2002). Hence the importance of infusing what we do in schools with equity, for if it is viewed as a separate initiative, giving it priority will prove difficult in the face of formal accountability systems.

The view of accountability espoused in this book is a much broader one, firmly linked to the purposes that are consistent with education in and for a democratic society. This view holds that, as educators, we are accountable for ensuring that all students are valued and supported in achieving success. McKenzie et al. (2008) describe the need for a two-pronged approach. On one hand, we need to work toward improving a system that marginalizes students through the use of narrow measures based on standardization. At the same time, we need to recognize that these measures are the "currency of success" at the present time, and therefore ensuring that all students achieve by these standards in order to move forward remains a priority.

INCLUSIVE LEADERSHIP

Fostering inclusive leadership requires that we reconceptualize leadership as a collective process, rather than seeing it as embodied in the role of an individual leader. Ryan (2006) describes inclusive leadership as having two essential components. First, he considers leadership to be communal rather than being embodied in charismatic, gifted, or powerful individuals. In this view,

> all members of school communities are involved or represented in equitable ways. The process itself is inclusive in that everyone has a right to contribute. The ends for which it strives are also inclusive. They are geared to work for inclusive, just, and democratic schools and communities. (Ryan, 2003, p. 18)

In other words, inclusive leadership means ensuring that multiple voices are involved in the leadership process, and then ensuring that this collective works with intent toward creating more inclusive environments and programs. For example, there is no point in gathering together a diverse group of people only to have them work on activities like fundraising and deciding where to place the playground equipment. Rather, they could serve on committees that actively engage in finding ways to make families feel more included in school activities, or finding ways to expand the diversity of resources in the school, or working to involve students in community activities that broaden and enrich their understanding of diverse cultures and life situations.

Critical Consciousness

Inclusive leadership requires a commitment to developing and practicing critical consciousness. Ryan (2006) describes this process in the following way:

> Being critical means becoming more skeptical about established truths. Being critical requires skills that allow one to discern the basis of claims, the assumptions underlying assertions, and the interests that motivate people to promote certain positions. These skills enable people to scrutinize the evidence and the logic that proponents of a course of action employ to support their arguments and conclusions. Critical skills allow people to recognize unstated, implicit, and subtle points of view and the often invisible or taken-for-granted conditions that provide the basis for these stances. But critical consciousness involves more than just a set of intellectual skills. It also includes an eagerness to engage in this sort of critique and a willingness to follow through on positions. People who possess a critical consciousness have a desire not only to engage in critique but also to act in support of their views. (p. 114)

Engaging others in critical reflection, as in applying the questions suggested in this chapter, is no easy task for principals and teachers, in their full and often harried days. It is not a practice that is "efficient." However, if progress is to be made in unearthing and addressing the beliefs and practices that systematically impede the success of our marginalized students, critical reflection needs to become a habitual part of school life. The Reflective Activities throughout this book are designed to help school leaders integrate critical consciousness into the regular processes and routines of school life.

Putting Inclusive Leadership Into Practice

Focusing on leadership to create more socially just conditions for students and families who live in poverty, Portelli and colleagues' (2007) comprehensive study of students deemed to be "at risk" provided the basis for the national report entitled *Toward an Equitable Education: Poverty, Diversity, and Students at Risk.* Based on their findings, they offer recommendations for teachers and school administrators to enhance the achievement and school experience of students who are marginalized and struggling. These recommendations, outlined in the box below, make clear the centrality of equitable leadership in improving our success in meeting the needs of each student in our schools. Their suggestions provide an excellent summary of the foundational principles for equitable leadership discussed in this chapter.

Recommendations for Teachers and School Administrators

Work toward recognizing dominant norms, assumptions, values, and traditions (e.g., in terms of race, class, gender, sexuality, ability, spirituality) in schools and school systems, and the many and daily ways in which students at risk are marginalized by them.

Take seriously the multiple perspectives which students bring, creating genuine opportunities for them to contribute to school curriculum, practice, and policy.

Make deliberate and sustained efforts to develop classroom and school cultures in which it is safer for students to speak.

Examine all school practices and policies (e.g., discipline policies, safe schools programs, attendance policies, parental involvement practices, health policies) from the perspective of who benefits and who is disadvantaged, who is included and who is excluded by them, who is heard and who is silenced.

In the daily discourses of classrooms, schools, and school systems, encourage continuing explicit conversations about issues of power and privilege and how they work in schools to normalize the experiences of some and marginalize those of others.

Work toward creating collaborative school cultures in which democratic human relations are central. This implies reflecting on fads

(Continued)

(Continued)

of "corporatization," including legalistic, bureaucratic, and overly regulatory ways of operating, and the predominance of business and managerial discourses.

Aim for a curriculum of life that takes into account students' lived experience, their local and global concerns, and respects their intellectual capacities by maintaining high academic quality.

Broaden definitions of academic standards and quality to include multiple forms of knowledge, various ways of knowing, and demonstrations of knowledge as contested and co-constructed.

Include multiple and diverse forms of assessment; recognize the value of contextualized teacher evaluations and performance-based assessments.

Work toward making schools places where it is safe for administrators, teachers, parents, and students to disagree. Understand that disagreement and conflict are characteristic of democratic spaces, and not indications of disrespect or insubordination.

Allow for a variety of context-sensitive support structures such as alternative schedules, diverse programs, and flexible counselling arrangements to address the diverse needs of students.

Approach high poverty communities as resourceful and not as deficient or in need of remediation; in other words, *work with* rather than *do for* communities.

Source: From *Towards an Equitable Education: Poverty, Diversity, and Students at Risk— The National Report* (pp. 56–57), by J. Portelli, C. Sheilds, and A. Vibert, 2007, Toronto: Ontario Institute for Studies in Education. Reprinted with permission.

CHAPTER SUMMARY

In this chapter, we explored some of the underlying assumptions and principles that are foundational for work as an equitable educator and leader. We considered the centrality of democratic purposes of education. In order to advance our thinking about inclusive and socially just educational leadership, we looked first at how exclusion, oppression, power, and privilege operate. Acknowledging the difficulties of advocating for equity and inclusive education within narrow accountability systems, a description of inclusive leadership set the framework for discussing critical consciousness and for putting strategies into action to create more equitable and socially just schools.

Case Study: The Field Trip Plan

When Catherine arrived as the new principal of Casterbridge Elementary School, she was very much aware of that old advice to move slowly at first. Better to get to know the culture of the school and to avoid making dramatic changes right away. Casterbridge Elementary School was situated in the center of the city. In addition to serving the neighborhood population, who tended to struggle with issues of poverty, the school also hosted an Extended French program for students whose parents transported them largely from more affluent neighborhoods further away. Catherine knew from the outset that finding ways to integrate the students from these two different programs would need to be a priority.

During the first month of school, the teachers from each division submitted their collective plans for the upcoming year's fieldtrips. As she perused the plans, Catherine noticed that the neighborhood classes were scheduled to visit a few local attractions. The Extended French classes, however, had significantly more frequent and more costly ventures planned. The disparity was most evident in the plans for the Grade 8 end-of-year field trips. The neighborhood class was scheduled to go on a day trip to a nearby city. The plan for the Extended French Grade 8, on the other hand, was a four-day trip to Quebec City.

When Catherine approached the chairs of the divisions to ask about the glaring inequity of the plans, she was told that this was the way they planned trips every year. They did it this way, she was told, because "it wouldn't be fair to put pressure on neighborhood families to finance trips that they couldn't afford. Besides, the neighborhood classes also have more behavioral problems so it's harder to take them away from the school." Traditionally, the Extended French Grade 8 students went to Quebec in order to practice their French. "After all," Catherine was told, "it was a 'special program' and the parents would be furious if the field trips were reduced."

When Catherine said the plan would need to be reworked to create more equitable treatment of students in both programs, the backlash was severe.

Questions for reflection:

1. How has the language of caring and compassion been used to mask issues of power, privilege, and inequitable treatment at Casterbridge Elementary School? Have you encountered similar use of compassionate discourses in your school experience?

2. What would you do in Catherine's situation? What alternatives might create a more fair and cohesive treatment of all the students in the school?

3. How might Catherine help both teachers and parents look at the situation with the best interests of all students in mind? How might they collectively find ways to enrich the experiences of all students without burdening those parents who struggle with issues of poverty?

REFLECTION ACTIVITY

CampbellJones et al. (2010) offer a guiding question and set of sub-questions to interrogate directly how power, privilege, and systems of oppression—sexism, racism, classism, homophobia, ableism, religious discrimination—are operating in specific, regular school practices. Use these questions as an application of critical consciousness in thinking about your context.

> *Who benefits and who is at the margins based upon the dominant culture maintained by all members of the organization?*
>
> ❉ ❉ ❉
>
> - What are the patterns, rules, and regulations that govern you as you interpret your relationships with the children in your classroom?
> - What patterns are operational in your background and determine how you come to understand parents and the communities in which they live?
> - If your lifeworld experience is about educating *some* children to achieve well academically, how do you change these patterns, given that they shape the way you approach the very issue of educating *every child* to achieve?
> - Who benefits and who is at the margins based upon the dominant culture maintained by all members of the organization?
>
> ---
>
> *Source:* CampbellJones et al. (2010, p. 70).

PRINCIPALS' ACTION STEPS

SELF   Reflect upon some of the unquestioned regular routines in the school that might favor some groups and marginalize others.

OTHERS

View the video *Critical Issues in Equity and Inclusive Education: Part 1* (Ontario Principals' Council, 2010) at http://www.princi pals.ca/Display.aspx?cid=8194&pid=8075 with the administrative team and/or school improvement team and/or staff. Respond as a group to the Reflective Questions accompanying the video.

TRY TOMORROW

Choose two of the regular routines considered in the SELF activity above. Have a discussion with at least two colleagues in the school about the possible negative effects of these routines and how they might be remedied.

CHAPTER THREE

The Personal Journey

Janice Gould, Maidu Nation, has written, "I would like to believe that there are vast reserves of silences that can never be forced to speak, that remain sacred and safe from violation." I feel that these sacred silences are the places from which we write. That place that has not been touched or stained by imperialism and hatred. That sacred place. That place.

(Brant, 1994)

The challenges and obstacles that principals face around creating more equitable schools are immense. To truly embrace these challenges and clear these obstacles, principals need to look within, engage in a journey of personal reflection, and explore their social and cultural identities and the complexities of power dynamics in schools.

SOCIAL AND CULTURAL IDENTITIES

Social and cultural identities have become increasingly ambivalent, ambiguous, and tremulous. Stuart Hall's dialogue on the subject of cultural identity and representation makes it clear that identity is not an accomplished fact. He suggests that "we should think, instead, of identity as a 'production,' which is never complete, always in process, and always constituted within, not outside representation" (Hall, 2006, p. 233). What research into social and cultural identity reveals is that most individuals begin as "something" and are then constantly changed into "something else" (a *changing same*) as the self is understood in relation to "Others" (positioning) and becomes involved in social action (activism).

The purpose of this chapter is to initiate an awareness of this process and demonstrate how social and cultural identities influence our commitment to, and practice of, inclusive and democratic education. Every principal of an equitable school should know and understand how aspects of their identities directly and indirectly affect their leadership perspectives, attitudes, behaviors, and, most important, their dedication to improved student achievement and authentic engagement with the entire school community. Students, teachers, and parents need to know who the principal is as well as what the principal does.

(DE)CONSTRUCTING NARRATIVES

The work on narrative inquiry by Clandinin and Connelly (2000) talks about the power of story and the importance of understanding one's own narrative before engaging with the narratives of others. They would argue that the meaning-making we do of events and people around us is based on our own stories and experiences. We see life, events, and people through our own lenses and make judgments, conclusions, and predictions based on our own experiences. This is why, as educators, it is important to access our own stories and reflect on our lived experiences by probing them more deeply. For example, as a young person of color, you may have experienced racism growing up in a predominately White community. The experience of being teased based on the color of your skin would have tremendous impact on how you view the world, events, and people. If the racial identity of students of color is not validated during their formal education, they may lose confidence and not see themselves as being able to achieve at the same level as their White counterparts. If students of color have never been exposed to role models of excellence in positions of responsibility, they may be unable to see themselves in such roles.

Hannum (2007) notes that "our social identity, and that of others, has the power to *bind* or to *blind* us." For a person from the majority culture, it may be evident in the activity of hiring a staff that reflects the mainstream culture, rather than reflecting the diverse school community. If school leaders do not take the time to acknowledge and reflect on such experiences, they may not realize the impact of their actions on students. How many times have we seen people who have been hurt by their past experiences and the resulting anger that may negatively impact their current relationships? In the case of educators, students may be the recipients of the negative impact.

Let us consider the ways in which we often acknowledge students. Some of the affirmations that are provided, unintentionally, may negatively impact the students whom we serve. Do students who wear religious headgear feel as affirmed as other students? We hear comments made by educators to students about how nice a student's hair looks or how great the new haircut is. Have we heard teachers acknowledge how nice someone's hijab or the color of someone's turban is? The absence of such comments and the affirmation of other students who may not be part of the "other" can lead students of these religious groups to feel less valued than their peers. School leaders, faculty, and staff need to acknowledge their experiences and take time to analyze their personal stories. This is a critical precursor to engaging in equity and diversity work. An analysis of our own narrative will highlight certain stereotypes and biases that we adhere to due to our experiences. We all have such prejudices, but it is important to recognize that they are there and even more important to analyze how these experiences impact us currently. By acknowledging, understanding, and reflecting on our experiences and stories, we develop better habits of mind to acknowledge, understand, and reflect on the stories of the students and the communities we serve.

> Culturally proficient leadership is distinguished from other leadership approaches in that it is anchored in the belief that a leader must clearly understand one's own assumptions, beliefs, and values about people and cultures different from one's self in order to be effective in cross-cultural settings. (Terrell & Lindsey, 2009, p. 5)

STALKING OUR STORIES: UNEARTHING, UNRAVELING, UNDERSTANDING, AND UNFOLDING

Our stories are rich sites and sources for ongoing learning. Some of them even stalk us. In this chapter, we will unearth, unravel, understand, and unfold our and others' prior experiences with issues arising from race, ethnicity, class, gender, sexuality, and sexual orientation. These stories will serve as significant touchstones to reflect on and to construct a personal, cultural narrative to reveal each one of us as a *changing same*. Knowing ourselves in this way is the first step on the journey toward inclusive leadership. In order to truly make change as leaders, we must first look within and gauge where we are in our own personal journey and our own cultural narrative. This must happen before we can examine our schools and/or organizations from a more critical perspective.

My Story of Distance and Displacement

After all this time, I still think about this story. It was many decades ago. I'm leaving the Caribbean for the first time. I'm traveling to Britain for my first visit. My colonial girls' school education, with its clearly defined parameters, had been an exercise in an exclusive, specific, political, aesthetic, cultural context which was predominantly White, liberal, and middle class. The man sitting on the airplane is a stranger. We spend the whole trip engaged in pleasant conversation. Before disembarking, we exchange telephone numbers. I never expect to hear from him. He is White and English. I am Black and Guyanese. He is older and I am younger. Surprisingly, I do hear from him. I am flattered. I fail to even think about his reasons for wanting to see me again. We begin to date. I'm reminded by my mother that Black girls do not date men before and without having an opportunity to ask some form of bell hooks' grandmother's essential question: "Well, who are his people?" (hooks, 1990). I am unprepared for the stares and the whispers and even more unprepared, when we are out together, for the angry elderly who show their disdain for me by spitting and shouting out names such as "slag."

How did I unpack, unravel, and understand this experience? I was unable to do so for a long time. Yon (1995) and others have presented findings in which immigrant voices speak of not being conscious of "Blackness" until they are "Othered" following a transition to a society in which "Whiteness" dominates. This story reassumes resonance in this exploration of the issue of identity and the questions it evokes—questions around issues of race, class, ethnicity, and sexuality. Yon quotes a friend's pronouncement: "I did not have an ethnicity until I came to Canada." I did not have an ethnicity or a sexuality mediated by race until I left the Caribbean.

I learned from this brief liaison that I was viewed as an unpleasant and illegitimate intrusion into what was then a relatively homogeneous nation. It was soon very evident to me that Englishness did not include "Blackness." No wonder Paul Gilroy titled one of his books *There Ain't No Black in the Union Jack* (1991). I also received useful insights into how my "self" was produced and structured in a colonial setting and how that "self" embraced the colonizers' values and culture. Considering my story points to issues of power and knowledge and their centrality in the negotiation and production of identity in minority groups. My story is also an expression of the reliance of contemporary racism on unchanging discourses of racial, ethnic, and sexual difference that are entangled with the history of the idea of culture in modern society and that continue to be powerful catalysts for my work in equity and social justice.

Awakening and Awareness

Lorna Crozier, award-winning poet and university professor, tells her story of growing up in poverty and the omnipresent effects of that experience. As a preschooler, she was not aware that her family was poor. She tells it this way: "I knew I was different, but I thought I was advantaged because we had the junkiest yard in the street. We were the only rental family on the block, and my dad was a collector of old pipes and oil drums, and things that he hoped to sell. And so our yard was where all the kids gathered to play, because there was nothing that they could ruin." It was not until she started school that she had an awakening about poverty and social class. She recalls walking home from school with some Grade 1 kids and hearing one of them say, while pointing at her house, "I wonder who lives in that poor house?" Crozier describes feeling as though she had been kicked in the heart, not answering truthfully, walking past her house, doubling back later and thinking, "My god, I am what they call poor." (Crozier, 2011)

Unpacking her experiences has led Crozier to an understanding of poverty as not only about financial deficits but more about cultural deprivation—no books, no art, no music—and a lack of hope. These insights have inspired her activist work in disrupting the systemic "statistics only" discourse of poverty by revealing the faces of the poor and sharing their stories.

The following story illustrates how the scripts we are exposed to as children linger in their effects on our attitudes and responses.

Planting Fear and Uncertainty

Sarah tells the story of battling her upbringing when it came to respecting sexual orientations other than her own heterosexual one. She loved the color pink when she was young, and her parents often indulged her preference in the clothing purchases they made for her. In fact, even her bedroom, like many of her friends' bedrooms, was decorated in pinks and purples. Hence her confusion when her younger brother Jimmy's request to have a pink shirt was met with laughter and unease from her parents. Not only did they laugh, but they ignored his request. When he persisted a few days later, her father responded with, "No, everyone will think that there's something wrong with you." She later overheard her parents talking heatedly about it and didn't understand what her father meant when he said, "Everyone will think he's a faggot." The tone of authority in his voice sent her the message that there was no room for questions or discussion.

Throughout her adolescent years, Sarah felt uncomfortable and avoided any discussion of gays and lesbians. This was often easy to do, as during those early years the topic was taboo at home and at school. She even avoided inviting a classmate whom she knew was gay to a gathering at her house for fear of her father's reaction.

(Continued)

(Continued)

Years later, as her awareness and understanding of differing sexual orientation grew and even when she became involved in activities that promoted gay rights in university, those early experiences still haunted Sarah. It was easy to unpack the experience cognitively, but for a long time she was left with the emotional twinge of fear and apprehension about LGBTQ issues, left as a scar from that childhood experience.

Sarah's story is a common one. For a long time she simply avoided addressing an equity issue by maintaining a silence about it and avoiding any possibility of raising it as an issue. Similar are the stories of parents who used to take their children across the street rather than walking by someone with a physical disability in order to avoid their children's embarrassing questions. It is one thing to address equity issues on a cognitive level, but it is essential that we address the very personal and emotional baggage that we carry as a result of our upbringing. Unpacking our stories in this way helps us to recognize what may encumber us in breaking the silence that surrounds all of the embodiments of difference in our schools and in society.

Stalking Our Stories, Knowing Our Selves #1

In Search of "Self"	Have you been marginalized?
Unearth	Think back to an incident or situation when you were marginalized by an individual/group/institutionalized situation.
Unravel	On what basis were you marginalized (race, gender, . . .)? How did the event take place?
	How did you feel/respond/react?
	When did you recognize the oppression (on the spot, much later)?
Understand	Why did you feel/respond/react in this way?
	How were you disempowered?
	What were the short- and long-term effects?
	What overt or subtle oppression was at play?

In Search of "Self"	Have you been marginalized?
Unfold reconsidered attitudes, responses, behaviors	How would you respond if this were to happen again/ continue? What positions of empowerment might you employ?

When we are deliberate in unpacking our stories in this way, rather than leaving them solely as uncomfortable memories, we grow in our ability to understand our own conscious and unconscious responses to others. Particularly important to the process above is the attention given to the feelings and emotions that accompany such experiences, as these affect the core of our being. If your experience involved one or a combination of particular "isms," you might try to generalize what you gleaned from this process to other "isms" that are not a direct part of your experience.

ACKNOWLEDGING YOUR POWER

One of the most engaging aspects of Laura Crozier's story is her struggle to attend university over the objections of her mother, who urged her to take a secretarial course instead. It would appear that Crozier's mother, as a result of her prior experiences, had adopted behaviors and practices that typify systemic oppression as discussed in earlier chapters. Many students who have been minoritized, whether by race, class, gender, and/or ability, speak of the ubiquitous power of teachers' expectations on learning and performance. They tell stories of the enduring adverse effects of streaming and tracking and the struggles involved in intervening and disrupting that harmful trajectory.

Briskin (2001) has found that there is a "hidden" curriculum about power that interrupts both teaching and learning. Within the Cultural Proficiency Continuum and the six levels of workplace cultural proficiency that were introduced in Chapter 1 (Figure 1.2), we are able to see in the first three levels—cultural destructiveness, cultural incapacity, and cultural blindness—examples of systemic discriminatory policies, practices, and behaviors. Principals and vice principals must therefore investigate the ways in which these power dynamics produce marginalization, exclusion, disempowerment, and silencing. Briskin suggests that "complex common-sense practices, moments and sites of power inform the classroom [and the school] in multiple ways" (p. 31). Here are some of these power dynamics for school leaders to reflect on.

Power Dynamics in Schools and Classrooms

- Patterns of authority and resistance
- Struggles about expertise and experience
- Control over access to knowledge
- Ways of evaluating student learning
- Structure and organization in the classroom
- Styles of conversation
- Classroom patterns of speaking and silence

Source: Adapted from Briskin (2001, p. 31.).

As you engage in your reflections, we encourage you to call up and interrogate situations in your school environment that may demonstrate how power is mediated in complex ways. As an individual, you may not be engaging in exclusionary practices, but by virtue of your position, you may be promoting inequitable and oppressive policies and practices. Marcus's story illustrates how this may occur.

Marcus's Story

Marcus had been a teacher at East Bay Secondary School in the 1980s for 11 years. He left to take a vice-principalship at another school and later returned to East Bay as principal. One of the responsibilities that he took most seriously in his early tenure was to ensure the success of the Grade 9 students on the new literacy test. A great deal of time and effort was spent on professional development for teachers and on encouragement and support for students. The school demographics had changed considerably during his absence, with a marked growth in the number of students of a Muslim faith. It wasn't until long after the test, when a parent from the Muslim community mentioned that the test had been conducted during Ramadan, a time of fasting, that Marcus realized the disadvantageous position these students had to face.

This story illustrates the ways in which we can be part of a system that creates barriers for students. The question for Marcus, once he was aware of the situation, was about what course of action he should take. He could decide that, although it was unfortunate for the Muslim students who observed Ramadan, "the system is the system," and it was his job to implement policy. As an equitable leader, however, raising this issue with senior administrators and advocating for a change in policy would better respect and serve the needs of his student and community population.

The following activity asks you to examine your role and your school/system's role in responding to difference and diversity.

Stalking Our Stories, Knowing Our Selves #2

In Search of "Self"	Have you or your school marginalized others?
Unearth	Think of a situation when you or your school were involved in marginalizing another person or group.
Unravel	On what basis did you, either intentionally or inadvertently, marginalize another person/group? How did you think/act inappropriately? When did you recognize/become aware of the oppression? What do you think the effects (short- and long-term) might have been on others?
Understand	Why might you have acted in this way (lack of knowledge, background experience, acculturation/ normalization . . .)
Unfold reconsidered attitudes, responses, and behaviors	How have/might your attitudes and responses change? What different actions would be appropriate?

Many of us can look back and identify times when we were part of systemic oppression such as the following:

- Implementing curricula with strictly Eurocentric perspectives
- Recommending career choices for students that reflected gender or social class stereotypes
- Referring students for special education support when their differences were cultural rather than cognitive
- Expecting less from students whose parents did not have postsecondary education

The value in unpacking these experiences in the manner suggested above is that we become more alert to the ways in which these forms of inadvertent oppression can occur. The process also makes it clear that we need to be open to suggestions from others who may see things that are invisible to us through our own narrow lenses. There is a much greater chance of unearthing and addressing systemic marginalization if we are deliberate in seeking out alternate viewpoints.

practical application for staff

AWARENESS AND REFLECTION

Increased awareness around one's personal cultural narrative can occur through activities that promote reflection on one's own personal experiences. At the end of this chapter, there are activities that allow individuals and groups of individuals to reflect on their personal narratives by highlighting their own biases and assumptions and exploring power dynamics. The activity entitled Forced Choice allows participants to acknowledge and reflect on their identities and think critically about how these identities may or may not have given them a position of power and/or privilege in society. One of the questions in this activity calls for participants to select one aspect of their identities, such as gender, sexuality, or race, that gives them the most power and privilege over others. It allows participants to then move to an area in the room with others who have chosen the same identity and talk about how their power and privilege in their chosen identity manifests in their relationships with others. When engaging in such activities, it is essential that there be a debrief, because it allows participants to surface personal and group assumptions and biases/stereotypes as well as issues of power and privilege. These types of activities generate healthy discussions about these issues. Furthermore, they allow groups to talk about their experiences from a critical stance and connect them to how these biases and assumptions are manifested in their relationships as educators in schools.

LEARNING FOR INCLUSIVITY AND COLLABORATION

As you considered the sample stories and situations above, insights about the influences that have shaped your beliefs, attitudes, and behaviors may have emerged. The following organizer is designed to help you construct a holistic profile that honestly reflects your perceptions about your cultural identity and how it has evolved. It asks you to consider the following aspects of cultural identity: class, gender/sexual orientation, race, ethnicity, language, religion, exceptionality, and physical context. In each of these areas, consider not only your own identity within the subculture but also what the relationship is between you and the dominant group within each subculture (bolded in each category). For example, if you are lesbian, how has your relationship with a dominant heterosexual culture influenced your identity? Or, if you are Black, how has your relationship with a dominant White culture influenced who you are as a person? It is also important to consider the influences between and among the different subcultures as well. For example, if you are Buddhist and living in a predominantly Buddhist community, that experience might be quite different from being Buddhist and living in a predominantly Christian community. Similarly, if you are First Nation or American Indian, your experience growing up on a reserve or reservation would be different from living in an urban center.

When you note that you are a member of the dominant group within a subculture, such as White, upper or middle class, and English speaking, consider the power and privilege that this has afforded you and how it affects your cultural identity. Finally, in each area, consider how your identity and relationships within this subculture have influenced who you are as a person and as an educator. The more detailed you are able to be in considering each of these areas, the richer your personal cultural profile will be. You may find it easiest to begin with the category that you perceive to have the greatest impact on you.

Building a Cultural Profile

Components of Cultural Identity	My Location, Relationships, and Experiences	Influences on My Identity as a Person and as an Educator
Class Below poverty line, homeless, working class, lower middle class **Middle class, upper class**	live in affluent area; able to experience a lot (w/ friends)	come in with experiences or things that others are awed by

(Continued)

(Continued)

Components of Cultural Identity	My Location, Relationships, and Experiences	Influences on My Identity as a Person and as an Educator
Gender/Gender Orientation **Male** Female **Heterosexual** Homosexual Bisexual Transgender		
Race American Indian/First Nation, Métis, Inuit **White** Black Asian Other		
Ethnicity **Western European** Central/Eastern European Latino Asian African Caribbean Other		
Age Child Youth **Young adult** **Middle aged** Senior		
Language **English** Bilingual (including English)		

Components of Cultural Identity	My Location, Relationships, and Experiences	Influences on My Identity as a Person and as an Educator
English as a second language Multilingual Non–English speaking		
Religion **Christian (Protestant)** Christian (Catholic) Christian (other, e.g., Mormon) Jewish, Islamic, Hindu, Buddhist Other		
Physical Context Urban, suburban, rural Geographic region Environment (coastal, mountains, prairies, desert)		

The activities described above are meant to help unpack our personal stories and interrogate the impact these may have on our daily practices, in the policies we develop and implement, and in the relationships that we develop in working with others. We can use these experiences to help us apply a critical consciousness in challenging our own expectations and assumptions. Consider, for example, the following scenario:

You are a part of a teacher hiring team spending a day interviewing candidates. The majority of the team members are White, and over the course of the day, you notice that they always are drawn to the candidates who are also members of the dominant culture. You are very much aware that the vast majority of the students in your area do not see themselves represented among the teachers and administrators in the school. During the course of the day, you hear comments such as the following:

"She has an accent."

"He might need accommodations for his religion."

"If she needs a cane to walk, how will she ever manage a class and handle recess?"

"The parents in our school are very religious and will give a teacher who appears gay a hard time."

How might the process of "stalking your own stories" suggested in this chapter assist you in responding?

How might you navigate these conversations to ensure that respect can be established and basic human rights are not compromised?

CHAPTER SUMMARY

This chapter focused on the self and the inner work necessary to move forward on the personal journey to being more equitable and inclusive in our work. This was deemed to be essential, for as Kose (2009) points out, "It is unlikely that principals can lead for social justice without engaging in ongoing self-examination; developing networks of difference, hope, support, and critique; and continuously deepening and reconnecting with the passion, courage, and responsibility of truly serving all students (p. 656). Following several examples, an invitation was extended to use a framework to "stalk our own stories" by *unearthing, unraveling,* and *understanding* personal stories of individual/group and systemic oppression and, as a result of this process, to *unfold* reconsidered attitudes and responses.

Case Study: An Early Story of School

I was born in 1973 to immigrant South Asian parents in Vancouver, British Columbia. I was raised in a small urban community where diversity in race was limited to a handful of Black families and a small community of about five South Asian families, my family being one of them. My earliest recollections of this go back to kindergarten, when as a five-year-old, I was asked to draw a picture of my family. My family consisted of an extended family that included my parents, my brother, my aunt, my uncle, my two cousins, and my grandparents. This was the only notion of family I knew when I first started school.

But then the teacher asked me to draw my family. I had never seen or heard of a family like mine. I liked my teacher and I wanted her to like me, too.

So I decided that I would draw my family the right way—a mom, a dad, and a brother, knowing full well that my picture did not depict my true family. I had excluded a number of people who were a part of my family. I felt disappointed in myself because I knew when I took the picture home I would hurt the feelings of my excluded family members. And I did. But, I gave the teacher the right answer. The books all showed white faces with a mom, a dad, a brother, and a sister. I played "family" in the kitchen play center in kindergarten as well, and I knew what family was all about because school told me so.

As I moved into Grade 5, I became one of the popular kids, because my brothers (my biological brother and my two male cousins) and I were heavily involved in competitive sports such as soccer and basketball. For the most part I remember being in a happy and comfortable space during this year. However, I do remember clearly an issue that came up in class. From the time that I started school to Grade 5, I do not remember seeing one person in the resources, textbooks, and the staff of the school that looked like me. The first time I saw someone who looked like me was on the cover of a Language Arts reading textbook. When the textbook was handed to me, I looked into the face of a girl who somewhat resembled me. She had black, braided hair, dark eyes, and a brown complexion. I felt embarrassed because I knew what was going to come next by my fellow students. As soon as they saw the textbook, many of them commented by saying, "Look—Samira's on the cover of the book." Many laughed. I wanted to hide, and I wished so much that the textbook did not exist, or if it did exist, it didn't have a picture on the cover of a girl who had a face like mine. For the rest of the year, I hoped that the dreaded textbook would not come out. It did, and each time I relived the anxiety and embarrassment of the last time.

Guiding Questions for Discussion

1. How do notions of what is "personal" come to be constructed?

2. How do you negotiate a space for the "other" in your classrooms and schools?

3. What was considered "normal" when you were in school that has now been contested?

4. Whose narrative and/or voice was evident in these classrooms? Whose voice was missing?

REFLECTION ACTIVITY

Objective

For the most part, we do not examine or interrogate the various aspects of our identity, the intersectionality of our identities, power and privilege derived from identity, or the impact of identity in our daily lives. This activity is designed to challenge participants to think about their own identity while making connections and sharing with others. This activity can also be extended to start a dialogue with educators about their students' identities and how educators perceive and respond to issues of identity.

Materials Needed

- Laminated identity signs: race, gender, socioeconomic class, sexual orientation, immigration status, ability/disability status, religion, age
- Masking tape

Setup

Post the eight identity signs around the perimeter of the room so that they are accessible to the group moving to them.

Facilitation Directions

1. Ask the group to come together in the center of the room for instructions.

2. Explain that there are two parts to this activity: One is a silent/reflective part when we are together in the center of the room; the other one is a sharing part that will take place once everyone has made a choice with respect to each of several statements.

3. Explain that you are going to read an incomplete statement and that each person will choose one of the eight parts of their identity to complete it. All group members should be encouraged to self-reflect and choose for themselves where they will go in the room. Emphasize that this is the silent part.

4. Once participants have made their individual choices, ask them to share in small groups of three or four why they selected that part of their identity to complete the statement.

Allow for several minutes of dialogue, and then ask them to return (silently) to the center of the room.

5. Read aloud another incomplete statement, and repeat the process above.

6. Sample statements:
   o The part of my identity that I am most aware of on a daily basis is _____.
   o The part of my identity that I am the least aware of on a daily basis is _____.
   o The part of my identity that was most emphasized in my family growing up was _____.
   o The part of my identity that I would like to explore further is _____.
   o The part of my identity that serves as my primary compass for my work style is _____.
   o The part of my identity that garners me the most privilege is _____.
   o The part of my identity that I believe is the most misunderstood by others is _____.
   o The part of my identity that I feel is difficult to discuss with others who identify differently is _____.

Debrief

- Discuss what the activity was like to do. (People often say that they didn't realize how much they have in common with one another or that they were surprised about how they answered the questions.)
- Build on the comments that may address that it was difficult or that participants don't often think about all the parts of their identities.
- Discuss thinking about self and the impact our identities have on our being educators, leaders, et cetera.

Modification

In using this activity, I noticed that some people had difficulties making a choice. The reasons included these:

- They didn't know where to go.
- It was difficult having to choose, because more than one identity applied.

- They had not thought about their identity in the way framed by the questions.
- The identity they would have chosen was not listed.

For these reasons, I created a "neutral zone" back in the middle of the group, where people could stay. I encourage people to talk about why they found themselves in this zone.

I would not be inclined to add other identities, unless there is a particular issue that needs to be discussed or examined by the group. I think that it makes for a richer examination and dialogue in the debrief if participants make these observations or connections or if the facilitator is able to further challenge participants through additional questions.

Source: Retrieved and adapted from *Teampedia,* http://www.teampedia.net/wiki/index .php?title=Forced_Choice. This work is licensed under the Creative Commons Attribution-NonCommercial-ShareAlike 2.5 Generic License. To view a copy of this license, visit http:// creativecommons.org/licenses/by-nc-sa/2.5/ or send a letter to Creative Commons, 444 Castro Street, Suite 900, Mountain View, California, 94041, USA.

PRINCIPALS' ACTION STEPS

SELF	Engage in exploring your own narrative/ experiences, and reflect on your own identity in terms of race, gender, class, sexuality, and religion. Ask yourself how these identities give you power and privilege in your interactions with others.
OTHERS	View the video *Leading the Inclusive School, Part 1: The Personal Journey* (Ontario Principals' Council, 2010) at http://www.principals .ca/Display.aspx?cid=8194&pid=8075 with your administrative team and/or school improvement team and/or staff. Respond as a group to the Reflective Questions accompanying the video.
TRY TOMORROW	Use one of the activities at the end of this chapter with your staff.

CHAPTER FOUR

Creating a School Climate That Promotes Equity

In the end, it comes down to a question about the purpose of public schooling and its role in a democratic society, about what we want for our children and their futures. Do we as citizens, as educators, parents, and caring members of society, value a strict and disciplinary conformity . . . or do we instead accept the imperatives of freedom, equality, diversity, opportunity, and justice.

(Vinson, Gibson, & Ross, 2001)

O ne of the activating "stories" in the book *Beyond the Bake Sale: The Essential Guide to Family-School Partnerships* by Henderson, Mapp, Johnson, and Davies (2007) is titled "The Counter." Steve Constantino tells the story of his first day as a high school principal in Virginia. He enters the main office. The carpet is worn, the plastic chairs don't match, and the clocks tell the wrong time—and then there is the counter, fifteen feet long and four feet high, covered with peeling laminate and acting as a barrier between the school and all those who dare to enter. Behind the counter are the tops of two heads. After clearing his throat a few times and repeating "Good morning," one of the heads asks, "Yes?" Steve later learns that she is the receptionist. "I'm the new principal." "Oh, your office is over there." She points and goes back to "work." That afternoon, the counter is removed forever.

The ways in which schools define and present themselves profoundly affect the social attitudes, interactions, behaviors, and learning of all students and the schools' relationships with all stakeholders. The school administration and staff are highly visible to all members of the school community. Through their attitudes and dispositions, the school staff models expectations for the entire school community. The message in Steve Constantino's school was this: Don't disturb our universe; you are not welcome here, but if you dare to come in here, we'll get to you when *we* choose and get you out of here with the least amount of interaction and communication. Such a response dishonors the principles of equity and inclusive education. A positive and inclusive school climate is one where all members of the school community should feel safe, welcomed, and accepted. The Ontario Ministry of Education (2009a) defines school climate as "the sum total of all the personal relationships within the school. Every person within the school community is entitled to experience a positive school climate, free from discrimination and harassment" (p. 27).

SCHOOL CLIMATE AND LEADERSHIP

In the last three decades, a growing body of research has confirmed the link between the school learning climate and students' academic achievement and healthy development. Quoting from a number of researchers, Sanders and Sheldon (2009) state that school climate is "associated with leadership style, sense of community, expectations for students, an ethos of caring and a variety of student outcomes" (p. 19). In our view, school climate is also very closely linked to inclusive leadership and social justice leadership. In Chapter 2, we provide a comprehensive presentation of what inclusive leadership means. In brief summary, inclusive leadership means this:

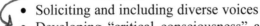

- Soliciting and including diverse voices
- Developing "critical consciousness" and integrating it into school practices
- Working toward inclusive ends (Ryan, 2006)

Improving the climate of learning for all students is unattainable without the attributes of an inclusive leader. Such leaders are imbued with the characteristics of social justice leadership, which Theoharis (2007) defines as "principals who make issues of race, class, gender, disability, sexual orientation, and other historically and currently marginalizing conditions in the United States central to their advocacy, leadership practice, and vision" (p. 221). Principals cannot do this work alone. They must understand how to work with an existing culture and must also know how to help it evolve into a healthier one. The disappearance of the counter in Steve Constantino's school is symbolic of the beginning of a change in that school's climate and culture. The principal, using a range of equity frameworks and reflection tools, must lead all stakeholders in creating a vision and clear action plans for promoting a safe, secure, supportive learning climate. Some of the attributes of a supportive climate in successful schools are these:

Continual Sharing of Ideas: Teachers share ideas daily with each other and with their students and families regarding vital issues of instruction, curriculum, testing, school organization, and the value of specific knowledge.

Collaboration: Teachers become involved in team teaching and other collaborative efforts in program development, writing, and research, including action research.

Egalitarianism: Teachers dispense with formalities, and anyone can vote who, for example, takes an interest in a department meeting. The notion is that the quality of ideas is more important than the source.

Practical Application: Teachers ask themselves: How does what we are doing help students, teachers, and schools? What did we do this week to help?

Leadership From Principals: Principals who desire to improve a school's culture must foster an atmosphere that helps teachers, students, and parents know where they fit in and how they can work as a community to support teaching and learning. Creating a school culture requires instructional leaders to develop a shared vision that is clearly communicated to faculty and staff. Additionally, principals must create a climate that encourages shared authority and responsibility if they are to build a positive school culture.

Source: Adapted from MacNeil and Maclin (2005).

School leadership, second only to teaching, is the primary determinant of successful student learning and achievement. The principal plays a major role in articulating goals and expectations for all partners in developing an effective school. School climate is a significant element in efforts to improve academic performance and school transformation. School climate affects the process of teaching and learning; certain aspects of school climate can also support learning while others can impede learning. Each of us must ask and reflect deeply on questions such as the following:

- Is the *physical environment* welcoming and conducive to learning?
- Does the *social environment* promote communication and interaction?
- Is there an *affective environment* that promotes a sense of belonging and self-esteem?
- Does the *academic environment* promote learning and self-fulfillment?

Continuous school improvement requires principals to demonstrate shared and committed leadership by supporting "the active engagement of students, parents, federations and unions, universities and colleges, service organizations, and other community partners" (Ontario Ministry of Education, 2009a, p. 17). These groups, working collaboratively, can develop positive school cultures through regular monitoring, assessment, and analysis. To engage in these processes requires careful and conscientious data collection. School climate surveys that incorporate questions on equity and inclusive education are a most useful tool for gathering data on school culture.

In Ontario, the Safe Schools Action Team (2005) recommended that schools conduct a climate assessment to collect student, staff, and parent perspectives on safety. The surveys are to be used to help in-school teams determine school needs and make decisions on school climate and bullying-prevention programming. Sample climate surveys are now available at http://www.edu.gov.on.ca/eng/teachers/climate.html.

Formal surveys can be conducted at the school level or classroom level and should involve students, staff, parents, community members, and school administrators. The data collected should be used to begin a dialogue among the school's stakeholders for the purpose of moving toward meaningful change. Informal assessments are usually conducted within a school using checklists administered by school staff members. These scans can provide a wide range of formative information on academic and nonacademic aspects of school life and can be used to direct school improvement efforts. Cohen, Pickeral, & McCloskey (2008/2009) describe school climate data as offering a new kind of accountability, one that gets to the heart of what schools are for:

> When we use only academic achievement data to understand learning and school improvement efforts, we are ignoring a fundamental truth: The goals of education go far beyond linguistic and mathematical learning. Today, more and more districts, states, and networks of schools are using school climate data to help define school success. We believe that this is a substantive step forward for public education—one that supports the whole child and the whole school community. ("A New Kind of Accountability," para. 4)

They also acknowledge that, in addition to being developed in a scientifically sound manner, school climate assessments must meet two very significant criteria. They must

1. recognize student, parent, and school personnel voices; and

2. assess all the dimensions that color and shape the process of teaching and learning and educators' and students' experiences in the school building.

They further cite the Center for Social and Emotional Education's (CSEE, 2009) Comprehensive School Climate Inventory as a top tier instrument for systematic measurement in the four areas that shape school climate—safety, relationships, teaching and learning, and the institutional environment. You will find more information on this survey at http://portal.schoolclimate.net/.

SCHOOL CLIMATE AND FAMILY AND COMMUNITY PARTNERSHIPS

There is recognition among educators that partnerships among schools, families, and community groups are a necessity. Partnerships have a positive impact on school climate and school improvement, and the benefits to staff and students are immeasurable in terms of learning opportunities. Parent engagement, particularly, has a profound impact on student attitude and attendance and on closing the achievement gap.

Pushor and Ruitenberg (2005) believe that parent engagement is not about what leaders have to do; it is about what leaders get to do: It is

> about moving inward to look closely at your assumptions and beliefs, both individually and collectively with others; to be both a host and a guest on a school landscape; to build trust and relationships with parents. It is about what you have the chance to do—to make a difference in the lives of children and their parents as you work alongside them in the important work of teaching and learning. (p. 69)

In this type of school environment, parents and community members are engaged and welcomed as respected and valued partners. The climate within such a school setting encourages and includes the active participation of diverse voices, including those of underrepresented peoples. Leaders reaching out to the underrepresented members of the community will have a positive impact on learning for all students. It also encourages school personnel to educate themselves about the cultural, racial, and faith parameters that exist within their schools. Henderson et al. (2007) have developed a comprehensive checklist and excellent exemplar survey: How Family-Friendly is Your School? (pp. 75–79). Chapter 7 in the present volume provides a deeper exploration of the benefits of family and community partnerships to school improvement.

SCHOOL CLIMATE AND EXPECTATIONS FOR STUDENTS

In earlier chapters we reported that schools work well for certain groups of students, while many others are underserved. The Ontario Ministry of Education defines curriculum as everything that surrounds the student in the learning environment, not just what the teacher points to. In a study completed by William Preble and others (as cited in Preble & Taylor, 2008/2009),

> Many students are subjected to aggressive, uninterrupted, verbal abuse every day.

Schools are full of injustice toward certain students who are viewed by their peers as being "different."

One in five students does not feel safe at school.

Some students leave school every day frustrated and angry because of their mistreatment by peers, and, in some cases, adults in the school.

More recently, Preble and Taylor (2008/2009) reported that their experiences with involving students in collaborative action research around school climate showed huge differences between adult and student perceptions:

> When teachers or principals perceive their schools to be safe and respectful places, they may be blind to problems going on right under their noses—and therefore be unresponsive. Students repeatedly tell us, "School climate is what happens when grown-ups are not around." (p. 36)

These findings reflect some of the evidence found by Craig and Pepler (1998) in their work on bullying when teachers, who were engaged in active playground supervision, failed to notice numerous acts of bullying taking place in full view.

Preble and Taylor's (2008/2009) "blind spots" research also revealed that the school climate data showed striking gaps between the perceptions of college-bound students and other students and equally dramatic disparities between teachers' and students' perceptions of school climate. These conclusions remind us that we must continue to be vigilant about the "cult of normalcy," as previously discussed, and be sure to ask ourselves: What data are right in front of us that we are not seeing or not able to see?

Goleman (1985) observes that

> there is a particular paradox when it comes to confronting those ways in which we do not see. To put it in the form of one of R.D. Laing's "knots,"

> > The range of what we think and do
> >
> > is limited by what we fail to notice.
> >
> > And because we fail to notice

that we fail to notice

there is little we can do

to change

until we notice

how failing to notice

shapes our thoughts and deeds. (p. 24)

The Ladder of Inference (Figure 4.1), initially developed by Chris Arygis and subsequently presented by Peter Senge, Art Kleiner, Charlotte Roberts, Rick Ross, and Bryan Smith (1994) in *The Fifth Discipline Fieldbook: Strategies and Tools for Building a Learning Organization,* is a very helpful tool in deconstructing Goleman's theory, which compels us to remain conscious about how we are performing in our environments and keeps us conscious of biases that we may not even be aware of.

This model takes us from a place of observable data to the point of taking action. Along the way, we select and deselect data, sometimes not even seeing obvious things. This is a consequence of something that we all do well, which is to focus our attention. Psychologists Christopher Chabris and Daniel Simons (2010) describe this phenomenon as the "illusion of attention" when we are unaware of how much we are not seeing. However, what is more disconcerting is that we interpret the data that we have selected and give meaning to them through our existing mental models and form conclusions that may or may not be accurate. We then use this meaning, based on personal and cultural experiences, to strengthen or shape our beliefs and act consistent with the beliefs that we have formed. These beliefs are so powerful that they affect the data that we select the next time around. To become more noticing, we need to change our intuitions, our instinctive beliefs, to know that we are not seeing everything. Therefore, school leaders need to ask themselves: With what experiences can I build my repertoire of skills? With what tools and models do I organize my thinking? What am I trying to accomplish? What am I failing to notice that I should notice? Reflecting on these kinds of questions moves schools from looking only at test scores as an indicator of positive school culture and climate toward a broader view and

Figure 4.1   Ladder of Inference

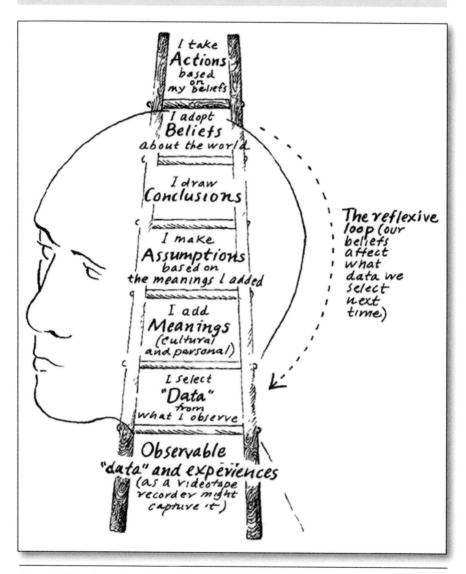

Source: Ladder of Inference, by Chris Argyris, as shown in Senge et al. (1994).

grander plan for developing more respectful and supportive learning environments, and toward recognizing the need to support and promote equity-minded student leadership.

SCHOOL CLIMATE AND STUDENT OUTCOMES

We know that school climate is composed of a complex set of elements. We know that it promotes meaningful student learning. The school and classroom climate clearly supported the learning and leadership of the Grade 11 Muslim student in Chapter 1, who intervened to bring an additive and corrective orientation to Islam to the approved text book in use in her history classroom. We also know that the school curriculum is multifaceted. Nora Allingham, former director of the Antiracism and Ethnocultural Equity Team, Ontario Ministry of Education and Training, itemized the scope and nature of the curriculum by reminding us that it includes the following:

- Seating plan
- Group work
- Posters
- Music
- Announcements
- Prayers and readings
- Languages spoken in the school
- Food in the cafeteria
- Visitors to the classroom
- Reception of parents in the office
- The race(s) of the office staff, custodial staff, administration, and teaching staff
- Displays of student work
- School teams, sports, and clubs
- The school logo or emblem
- Field trips

This is an important checklist, but even more important is how a list such as this should/could be used to rethink the existing formal curriculum, which still persists in foregrounding the values, experiences, achievements, and perspectives of European members of North American society. There are two Canadian secondary schools, for example, that had used the term "Redmen" to name their school teams that had to adopt new names for the teams and team logos out of respect for First Nations' experiences and perspectives. In addition to some of the entry points for implementing inclusive approaches to curriculum mentioned in Chapter 1, Zoric, Charania, and Jeffers (2003) put forward the following list of questions as a starting point for adapting existing curricular programs and practices:

- Whose voices are present? Whose voices are absent?
- What and whose knowledge is recognized? How is it recognized?
- Do resources acknowledge all people and perspectives?
- What assessment and evaluation tools will be most equitable?
- How do the social identities of teachers and other school staff shape interactions with students, parents, and community?
- How can we create a classroom and a school climate that supports and welcomes the diversity of all students, staff, and community members?
- How can the knowledge and experience of families and the general community be valued and reflected in our curriculum?
- Is a variety of methods used to ensure that all students are engaged in learning?
- Are students supported in their development as active citizens and leaders who are encouraged to advocate for social justice?

The questions cited in Chapter 2 and attributed to CampbellJones, CampbellJones, and Lindsey (2010) and Pollock (2008) also provide robust roots for reflecting on knowledge construction and transformation in the official curriculum. Rethinking curriculum therefore involves reworking content, altering pedagogies, examining issues of access, and creating a classroom climate that builds on the experiences of students and provides them with spaces to connect to their roots and their past and to envision the future.

Models such as the James Banks framework (Toronto District School Board, n.d.), which delineates both theoretical and practical approaches to inclusive curriculum, are informative about both process and progress toward total school community inclusion.

The James Banks Model—Approaches to an Inclusive Curriculum

Level 1	Contributions Approach	Adding diverse hero/ines to the curriculum selected, using criteria similar to those used to select mainstream hero/ines for the curriculum
Level 2	Additive Approach	Adding a variety of content, concepts, themes, and perspectives to the curriculum without changing its basic structure
Level 3	Transformation Approach	Changing the actual structure of the curriculum to help students to view concepts, issues, events, and themes from the perspectives of diverse groups
Level 4	Social Action Approach	Allowing students to make decisions on important social issues and take actions to help solve them

(See the Tools and Resources Section at the end of this book for a comprehensive description of this model.)

At Levels 1 and 2, students are passive recipients of information, and the curriculum remains virtually unchanged. Learning is teacher led and teacher driven with administrative support. It is at Levels 3 and 4 that there are opportunities for student leadership, where the students are active/activist learners who must develop a spirit of inquiry and engage in projects that promote and reflect equity. These approaches "aim for a curriculum of life that takes into account students' lived experiences, their local and global concerns, and respects their intellectual capacities" (Portelli, Shields, & Vibert, 2007, p. 57). Student-led clubs with a specific focus and issue-focused support groups such as Gay-Straight Alliances and Students and Teachers Against Racism (STARS) promote and encourage students to develop a positive school climate. Peer mediation models, where student leaders act as advocates around issues of harassment, human rights, and discrimination, are also powerful ways to engage students in their own learning and improve student outcomes.

CHAPTER SUMMARY

School leaders and school teams are using evidence-based data-driven decision making to guide school improvement efforts. However, discussions need to go beyond disaggregating standardized testing and assessments for learning data to also address the impact of school climate on student achievement. School climate is not an intangible; it deserves serious attention in the effort to improve student achievement. We need to ask ourselves: Am I responding to the physical, cultural, spiritual, emotional, social, and intellectual needs of the learner? And we need to be able to answer "yes" to all facets of that question. Careful and regular monitoring of school climate is an essential exercise in ensuring that we continue to remove all barriers to student learning and create a learning environment that is permeated with the principles of equity.

Case Study: Prevention Is the Key

During the lunch break, three male middle school students assault another student, Paul, who is a 13-year-old Black student who has experienced some academic challenges and has been harassed previously for acting effeminately. Paul is seriously injured, requiring medical attention. He requires numerous stitches for a facial laceration and has a broken nose.

The three students involved initially claim that Paul was making faces at them. They state that he looked at them in a funny way. Observers of the incident report that "Paul did nothing to provoke the assault" and was simply standing around watching all the students playing. No one heard Paul say anything to the other students who beat him up.

Incidents similar to this have occurred over the past three months, with this incident representing an escalation in severity.

1. Thinking about building a safe and caring learning environment, what specific strategies or ideas would you consider that would involve all key partners (students, staff, parents, community) at your school?

2. During the process of compiling your list of strategies/ideas with key partners, consider which action categories your strategies fall in. There may be overlaps and intersectionalities.

Strategies/ Ideas	Action	At the Classroom Level	At the School Level
	Already doing this . . . continue		
	Could do this easily		
	This will take time		
	This will be difficult		

REFLECTION ACTIVITY

If fish in the aquarium are sick—Don't blame the fish! Instead, check the water.

Center for Improving School Culture

A recent research brief from The Principals' Partnership mentions R. G. Owens and C. R. Steinhoff (1988) in Delisio (2006) who identified four distinctive school cultures, which we have renamed as follows:

- *One Big Happy Family:* A school that is a family or a team. The most important element is high regard and concern for each other, and total staff commitment to students and their culture is common.
- *Top Gear:* The school runs like a well-oiled machine. There is no collaboration. Everyone knows what to do and when to do it. The focus is on precision rather than nurturing learners.
- *The Dog and Pony Show:* A circus-type culture. The relationships and status in the organization come from theatrical practices. These schools are "all show and no go."
- *The Snake Pit:* The school culture is viewed as unpredictable. Tension and stress abound. People view it as a poison. They have no choice but to function or try to escape.

1. If a research team entered your school to monitor school climate, which attributes of these cultures would they discover?

2. Using an equity lens, describe the characteristics of your ideal school climate.

3. What strategies/processes would you put in place to achieve your ideal?

Characteristics of Current School Climate	Characteristics of Ideal School Climate	I/We will achieve our ideal in the following ways:

PRINCIPALS' ACTION STEPS

SELF — Review the responses to the reflective activity. Do a gap analysis to highlight the characteristics of the current school climate versus those of the ideal school climate.

OTHERS — View the video *Leading the Inclusive School, Part 2: Culturally Responsive and Relevant Pedagogy* (Ontario Principals' Council, 2010) at http://www.principals.ca/Display.aspx?cid=8194&pid=8075 with your administrative team and/or school improvement team and/or staff. Respond as a group to the Reflective Questions accompanying the video.

TRY TOMORROW — Select one area from The Centre for Urban Schooling's strategies for inclusive leadership discussed by Nicole West-Burns in the video—Curriculum and Classroom Climate, School Climate, Parent/Caregiver and Community Relations, Student Voice and Space, or Professional Development—and try one way to better reflect this strategy in your school community.

CHAPTER FIVE

Working With Staff

Another person's words are the windows to his or her world, through which I see what it is like to be that person. When another speaks to me in truth, he or she becomes a transparent self, and releases in me an imaginative experience of his or her existence. If he or she cannot speak, if I do not listen, or if I cannot understand then we must remain suspicious strangers to one another, uncognizant of our authentic similarities and differences.

(Sidney Jourard as cited in Style, 1996, para. 13)

Among the essential practices and competencies mentioned in many leadership frameworks for principals and vice principals is the ability to build relationships and develop people. Working in partnership with staff is vital to developing and sustaining the vision, commitment, and energy needed to nurture an equitable, inclusive, and antioppressive learning environment. Principals cannot do this work alone. In the previous chapter, we looked at strategies for developing and sustaining a positive school climate and culture. In this chapter, we explore some approaches to working directly with all staff on establishing effective channels of communication and the requisite skills and attitudes to infuse equity into the ethos of the school. Being strategic, establishing norms, and facilitating "courageous conversations" are central to this work. In addition, we also offer suggestions for understanding communication styles and for handling overt acts of harassment. Activities are suggested for teachers to examine culturally responsive pedagogy as well as their own expectations for student achievement. Finally, equity issues are raised as they relate to teacher supervision or teacher performance appraisal. Throughout all of these discussions, the intent is to provide principals with practical ideas for working directly with staff to keep everyone moving forward on the journey toward more equitable schools.

BEING STRATEGIC

There are some expectations for educational and personal interactions in schools that need to be nonnegotiable. One of these is a commitment to equity, inclusion, and antioppression. These stem from principles of human decency and are enshrined in supportive international, federal, state, and provincial legislation. For this reason, it is not sufficient to merely hope that teachers and all other staff will embrace this approach. It is necessary to develop an expectation that this is a nonnegotiable commitment. The alternative would be to continue to promote existing inequitable practices. It is not possible to be "neutral" on this front, for silence is one of the strongest actions in favor of the status quo. Teachers who advocate for the promotion of more inclusive, antioppressive schools need concrete evidence that they are supported in this work. Conversely, teachers who are reticent to take this stance need to know that they must be a part of activities that are intended to promote personal and professional growth in this area.

Ways to be concretely strategic in conveying this message include the following:

- Being explicit in the expectation that staff operate as a "community of inquiry" that is interdependent and responsible not only for their own learning, but for the collective learning of the group about issues of equity and inclusion
- Expressing beliefs and modeling behaviors that strongly convey the image of educators as agents of positive social change
- Expecting strategies for promoting equity and inclusive education to be embedded in teachers' annual plans. This does not mean including an "add on" component to their plans, but

providing evidence that equity, inclusion, and antioppressive methodologies are evident throughout curriculum planning and planning for extracurricular activities, and that these methodologies are contributing to the school/community environment

- Making equity and inclusive education a regular item for involvement in every staff meeting
- Expecting professional learning teams to incorporate direct equitable considerations and practices in their deliberations, plans, and implementation and evaluation strategies
- Institutionalizing the regular and ongoing questioning of individual, group, and system practices. The Equity Walk template provided in Chapter 8 can be used to engage in this process. The following set of questions, adapted from Ryan (2006), can be modified to examine how power and privilege might be embedded in both overt and subtle ways in the everyday life of the school:

Strategically Questioning Current Practices

- What is happening here? (e.g., "In this curriculum/choice of team members/assessment practice/weekly pizza days/discussion about parent involvement, what is happening?")
- Who says that this is the way things should be? (Are we doing this because it's "always been this way"? What has changed?)
- What overall purposes are being served?
- Whose vision is it?
- Whose interests are being served?
- Whose needs are being met or not being met?
- Whose voices are being silenced, excluded, or denied?
- Why is it that some viewpoints always get heard?
- Why is this particular initiative occurring now?
- What prudent and feasible action can we adopt to improve the situation?
- Who can we enlist to support us?
- How can we start now? How are we going to know when we make a difference?

Norms of Operation

Building relationships with staff that allow for deep discussion and personal investment requires the provision of norms that all can rely on to ensure that respect, privacy, and a safe environment will prevail. The following norms of operation provide an example.

Norms of Operation

Go slow to go fast: Taking time to ensure that everyone has a voice is essential. These are issues that cannot be dealt with efficiently.

Listen and speak with an open mind: Remember that others speak from a different set of experiences. This is the place to listen without judgment.

Take risks: It takes courage to raise and respond to issues that have traditionally not been part of staff meeting agendas. Rest assured that your comments/questions will likely resonate with others in the group as well.

Respect others and ourselves: Everyone has the right to be heard and to be imperfect. The aim is collective growth and understanding.

Leave positions at the door: There is no place for positional power in conversations about equity and inclusion. Everyone must be considered as equally able to contribute and to learn.

What we say here stays here: Respect for privacy is essential. These conversations are highly personal and require a firm commitment to keep the conversations in house.

Begin, end, and transition on time: This is important, because these conversations are draining and do not have obvious points of closure.

Source: Adapted from B. CampbellJones, 2008, Ontario Principals' Council Education Leadership Canada Symposium on Equity and Inclusion: Human Rights, Antiracism and Cultural Proficiency. Toronto. Adapted with permission.

These norms, or similar ones that better fit the particular context of your school, will facilitate progress in breaking down isolation in practice and discomfort in dialogue. All staff, including principals and vice principals, need to feel that they are an equal and integral part of a community of inquiry. As a principal, I recall a staff meeting in which we were discussing the importance of including literature and activities that allowed students in same-sex families to see themselves reflected in the curriculum. One teacher voiced the concern that this would raise backlash from segments of the school community. This provided the catalyst for a rich conversation about the conflict between personal religious beliefs and the need, in a public school system, to ensure that all students feel valued, included, and represented in the curriculum and school activities. It also led to a brainstorming of ways to productively and respectfully respond to parental concerns. (See "The Trouble With Penguins" at the end of Chapter 7 for a related case study.)

Modeling these general norms of operation in meeting contexts will also help teachers to develop strategies for creating classroom and school environments that are more inclusive, antioppressive, and conducive to maximizing the learning and engagement of all students.

FACILITATING COURAGEOUS CONVERSATIONS

In his study of the principal's role in professional development for social justice, Kose (2009) found that principals who were effective in this area "facilitated difficult and sensitive conversations" that fostered greater teacher responsibility for becoming aware of the ways in which oppressive beliefs and practices are institutionalized. This, in turn, had a positive impact on their ability to develop and implement strategies to better serve students who traditionally have been marginalized. According to Kose, these effective principals guided these conversations by providing evidence of achievement gaps; providing examples of both productive and harmful ways of meeting the needs of the underserved; demonstrating the courage to articulate examples of "their own unconscious racism; providing provocative videos that explored issues of race, class, and gender discrimination and identity construction; and conveying their own struggles and hopes for serving diverse students" (pp. 643–644).

Facilitating these discussions can be a difficult task. Some staff may wish to remain silent for fear of appearing discriminatory. Others may remain silent because of a long history of being misunderstood and undervalued. In their excellent resource for helping educators engage in the difficult task of unpacking and exploring their beliefs and attitudes about race, Singleton and Hays (2008) stress the importance of committing to the guidelines for having courageous conversations outlined in the box below. This is a strategy that was developed for

> breaking down racial tensions and raising racism as a topic of discussion that allows those who possess knowledge on particular topics to have the opportunity to share it, and those who do not have the knowledge to learn and grow from the experience. (Singleton & Hays, 2008, p. 18)

It is our suggestion that a similar approach would prove helpful in facilitating difficult conversations about other areas of difference, such as gender identity, sexual orientation, and poverty as well. A brief summary of each of these points is in order.

Four Agreements of Courageous Conversations

Commit to four points for engaging in, sustaining, and deepening dialogue about such issues as race, gender identity, poverty, and sexual orientation. We will

- stay engaged.
- speak our truth.
- expect to experience discomfort.
- expect/accept "nonclosure."

Source: Adapted from *Beginning Courageous Conversations About Race*, by G. Singleton and C. Hays, 2008, Thousand Oaks, CA: Corwin. Adapted with permission.

The following explanations expand the authors' intent in suggesting these commitments:

Stay engaged. The willingness to make a personal commitment to remain engaged in conversations that have traditionally been avoided is key. This engagement is both cognitive and emotional. Although silences do not necessarily indicate disengagement, the reasons for repeated silences need to be explored.

Speak our truth. Honest sharing of thoughts, feelings, and opinions is essential. People have a variety of reasons for avoiding honest expression, such as fear of being misunderstood or misinterpreted, fear of appearing angry or discriminatory, or fear of appearing ignorant or inexperienced.

Experience discomfort. Participants need to know up front that everyone will experience discomfort in these conversations, as we are not practiced in hearing and voicing perspectives that may not be part of the normalized way of talking about race (or poverty, sexual orientation, religious accommodation, etc.). It is important, however, to persist if we are to make progress in understanding and accepting the multiple perspectives that abound.

Expect/accept nonclosure. Because there are no easy solutions, no quick fixes, for these issues, there is a need to accept the fact that these conversations need to be ongoing.

CATALYSTS FOR DISCUSSION

Once guidelines such as the above norms and commitments have been established, finding catalysts to get these conversations started would be the next step. Several suggestions are provided below.

Personal Stories. Simply sharing personal stories about backgrounds and experiences that illustrate oppression or realizations about viewpoints that seemed "normal" to us in the past could be effective discussion starters.

Acknowledging Power Wheel. A good tool to use as a catalyst for beginning conversations would be the Acknowledging Power Wheel, illustrated in Figure 5.1. (See the Tools and Resources Section at the end of the book for a blackline master for this activity.)

In this activity, participants are asked to evaluate their position of power in relation to the dominant culture in each of the 12 domains. If they feel, for example, that their socioeconomic background has allowed them to feel and exercise power in society, then they would mark this section close to the center. Conversely, feeling/being marginalized or disempowered in this area would result in marking

Figure 5.1   Acknowledging Power Wheel

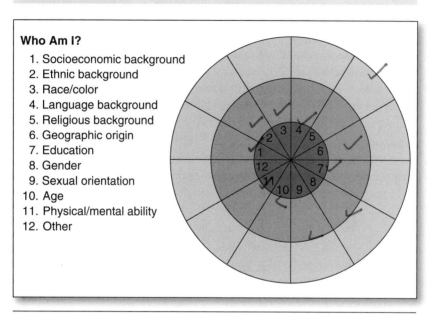

Who Am I?

1. Socioeconomic background
2. Ethnic background
3. Race/color
4. Language background
5. Religious background
6. Geographic origin
7. Education
8. Gender
9. Sexual orientation
10. Age
11. Physical/mental ability
12. Other

Source: Adapted from Lee (1992, p. 11).

toward the outside of the circle. Continuing in this way results in a personal profile of where we stand with respect to real and felt empowerment as a result of our gender, race, language, physical/mental abilities, et cetera.

Barriers to Inclusion Chart. The following chart might be used as a way of framing conversations either about our own experience of barriers or about particular students in the school.

Barrier to:	*General Example*	*Specific Example*	*Possible Intervention Strategies*	*Indicators of Success*
Feeling accepted				
Engagement				
Achievement				
Contributing to school community				

Film Clips. Film clips also provide a powerful way of seeing and viscerally experiencing individual and systemic inequities in action. Consider, for example, the film *Pretty Woman.* The treatment of Vivian Ward (played by Julia Roberts) in a high-end fashion shop when she is dressed in a miniskirt and high-heeled boots and considered "low class" contrasts sharply with her treatment when she enters as a well-heeled woman connected with a wealthy, powerful man in the community. Consider the treatment of Tom Hanks as a successful lawyer in *Philadelphia* before and after his boss discovers that he is gay and has contracted HIV. Consider the film *Freedom Writers* in which high expectations for racially marginalized and poor students, who had traditionally been written off as incapable of success, flourish under the influence of a teacher with high expectations. There are many films from which short clips can be extracted to be conversation starters about issues of discrimination and disempowerment. Key to the conversation would be making connections to the students with whom you work.

UNDERSTANDING COMMUNICATION STYLES

Working in partnership with school staff to develop an awareness of different communication styles that may be reflected in your school community will serve to promote equitable opportunities for students as well as more effective interactions with community members. It is important for educators to know that modes of communication are culturally constructed. In the dominant North American culture, for example, "active listening" is valued and expected as a way of letting people know that we are fully engaged in what the speaker is saying. In fact, as educators we are often trained in how to use active listening techniques, such as nodding our heads, maintaining eye contact, interjecting with positive reinforcement of what the speaker is saying, smiling, et cetera. In many other cultures, strategies to indicate fully engaged and respectful listening are quite different. For some indigenous cultures, maintaining eye contact would be considered bold and disrespectful, especially when the speaker is considered to be in a position of power. In some Asian cultures, engaged listening is characterized by a steady, full gaze with no expression or interjections.

Unfortunately, educators may misinterpret these latter modes of listening as signs that the listener is disinterested or does not understand what the speaker is saying. Developing the habit of

checking out assumptions and being open to learning about culturally constructed modes of communication is essential if teachers
are to be appropriately responsive to their diverse students, families, and community members.

DEALING WITH OVERT ACTS OF HARASSMENT

Educators need specific tools and strategies for dealing with overt
acts of oppression. The following strategy for dealing with harassment is one such helpful tool. It may seem counterintuitive to teachers used to the practice of reprimanding in private rather than using
the incident for public educative purposes. It is powerful in that it
helps to educate the victim, perpetrator, and witnesses about commitments to equity. It empowers the victim, holds the perpetrator
responsible for changed behavior, and holds all present responsible
for a renewed commitment to respectful treatment.

How to Handle Harassment
in the Hallways in Three Minutes

1. STOP THE HARASSMENT

   - Interrupt the comment/halt the physical harassment.
   - DO NOT pull students aside for confidentiality unless absolutely necessary.
   - Make sure all the students in the area hear your comments.
   - It is important that all students—whether onlookers, potential targets, or potential harassers—get the message that students are safe and protected in the school.

2. IDENTIFY THE HARASSMENT

   - Label the form of harassment: "You just made a harassing comment/ put-down based upon race/religion/ethnicity/abilities/gender/ age/sexual orientation/economic status/size (etc.)."
   - Do not imply that the victim is a member of that identifiable group.
   - A major goal is to take the spotlight off the target and turn the focus to the behavior. Students should realize what was said, regardless of what was meant (e.g., kidding).

(Continued)

(Continued)

3. BROADEN THE RESPONSE

- Do not personalize your response at this stage: "At this school, we do not harass people. Our community does not appreciate hateful/thoughtless behavior."
- Reidentify the offensive behavior: "This name calling can also be hurtful to others who overhear it."
- "We don't do put-downs at this school" specifically includes those listening, as well as the school community in general. Even if they were "only kidding," harassers must realize the possible ramifications of their actions.

4. ASK FOR CHANGE IN FUTURE BEHAVIOR

- Now turn the "spotlight" on the harasser, asking for accountability. Even if she or he was "only kidding," the harasser must realize the ramifications of the action. A major goal is to take the spotlight off the victim and turn the focus to the behavior. Students should realize what was said, regardless of what was meant (e.g., kidding). Personalize the response: "Chris, please pause and think before you act."
- Check with the victim at this time. "If this continues, please tell me, and I will take further action. We want everyone to be safe at this school." Again, be sure not to treat the victim as helpless or a member of any target group. Rather, plainly give her or him responsibility on behalf of others.

Source: Adapted from Equitable Schools: Gender Equity Resource Guide (p. 92), by Toronto District School Board, 2006, Toronto, ON: Author. Adapted with permission.

CULTURALLY RELEVANT AND RESPONSIVE PEDAGOGY

Helping each other as educators develop an understanding of the levels of cultural responsiveness that are manifest in different language and behaviors is a key part of making progress on the journey toward creating more equitable schools and communities. Stephanie Graham's chart, Six Levels of Workplace Cultural Proficiency, which was introduced in Chapter 1, provides a starting point and touchstone opportunity for engaging in this conversation. (See the Tools and Resources Section at the end of the book for a blackline master for this activity.) The chart provides explanations and examples of cultural responses, from cultural destructiveness at one end through cultural blindness to cultural proficiency at the other end. Self-reflection on this topic is essential in order for individuals to explore their personal beliefs, analyze their practices, and grow from what they discover there.

Personal Action Research

Personal action research is a private, hands-on way of collecting concrete evidence about one's own performance. Just as we often are unaware of personal idiosyncratic styles—such as repeating certain phrases, always sitting in the same chair in the staff room, or writing up our lesson plans in particular ways, teachers have "cultural styles" (Hilliard, 1989) that they may or may not be aware of. These styles may create an ethos of high expectations for all students, or they may, intentionally or more likely inadvertently, communicate high expectations for some and low expectations for others. In the following chart, Hilliard expresses his beliefs about the effects of teacher cultural styles on low-achieving students and provides a list of behaviors that research has indicated teachers with low expectations demonstrate:

Teachers and Cultural Styles by Asa G. Hilliard, III

The late Asa Hilliard III was a professor of urban education at Georgia State University and coauthor of *Saving The African American Child* (Hilliard & Sizemore, 1984).

❊ ❊ ❊

I remain unconvinced that the explanation for the low performance of culturally different "minority" group students will be found in pursuing questions of cognitive learning styles. I believe that the children, no matter what their style, are failing primarily because of systemic inequalities in the delivery of whatever pedagogical approach the teachers claim to master—not because students cannot learn from teachers whose styles do not match their own.

❊ ❊ ❊

(Continued)

(Continued)

There is a protocol of interactive behaviors of teachers who, for whatever reasons, have low expectations for students. Research in this area shows teachers tend to

- demand less from low-expectation students ("lows") than from high-expectations students ("highs").
- wait less time for lows to answer questions.
- give lows the answer or call on someone else rather than try to improve the lows' response through repeating the question, providing clues, or asking a new question.
- provide lows with inappropriate reinforcement by rewarding inappropriate behaviors or incorrect answers.
- fail to give feedback to lows' public responses.
- pay less attention to lows and interact with them less frequently.
- call on lows less often than highs to respond to questions.
- seat lows farther away from the teacher than highs.
- use more rapid pacing and less extended explanations or repetition of definitions and examples with highs than with lows.
- accept more low-quality or more incorrect responses from low-expectation students.
- in administering or grading assessments or assignments, give highs but not lows the benefit of the doubt in borderline cases.
- give briefer and less informative feedback to the questions of lows than to those of highs.
- use less intrusive instruction with highs than with lows, so that they have more opportunity to practice independently.
- when time is limited, use less effective and more time-consuming instructional methods with lows than with highs.

Source: Adapted from Hilliard and Sizemore (1984).

Teachers may use this chart to engage in some informal personal action research, in which they use a small pocket tape recorder or simply monitor the practices they use in interacting with the students in their classrooms. The aim would be to record a period of time in the classroom and then use the descriptors to analyze their own interactions with students as well as the planning and assessment practices that accompany the lessons recorded.

INCLUSIVE APPROACHES TO SUPERVISION

Inclusive leadership requires that we always stop to interrogate the position from which we are judging what it means to be a good teacher. How have our cultural predispositions shaped our notions about the attributes that contribute to effective teaching in a multicultural setting? Bell (2008) describes an experience in which she erroneously prejudged the effectiveness of a Black female teacher based on her culturally derived expectations of what was desirable teacher practice and then came to realize that her perspective had blinded her to alternate ways of bringing effective pedagogy to the classroom:

> How easy it is for those from dominant groups to judge others according to unexamined notions of what constitutes good teaching.[2] In this case, I unconsciously applied assumptions about good teaching based on an unacknowledged white and middle-class norm that could see only "warm fuzzy" teaching demeanors as good. I implicitly embraced a color-blind view of progressive pedagogy that did not take into account how educators who did not grow up white or middle-class might differently approach a pedagogy grounded in shared progressive goals but different prior schooling experiences. (p. 289)

Another example of this has been described by Delpit (1988). In her discussion she points out that most White middle class children are accustomed to being given directions in indirect and suggestive ways. Consider, for example, "Don't you think it's getting close to recess?" (meaning, "Put your work away and prepare to go out for recess"). Other cultures, including Black cultures, may not be accustomed to this inferential, roundabout style for giving directions. Using a more direct approach, which might be more beneficial for some students, may be judged as "too authoritative" by a member of the dominant culture, and may result in negative teacher appraisals that reflect more of a *cultural difference* than a *competency difference*. This is also critical to keep in mind when hiring staff to better represent the students and families in your school community.

Further, Bell (2008) points out that principals who go to the literature for support in how to conduct performance appraisals, and how to identify effective teaching, will find that the privileged position of dominant perspectives is supported, reinforced, and perpetuated in mainstream professional literature, simply because most of this professional research has been conducted by the dominant culture, using their lens through which to consider appropriate ways to communicate and interact in a learning context.

For this reason, when principals and vice principals are performing teacher appraisals, it is important to question their judgments of teacher *competence* by asking whether or not what they are observing is more a reflection of *culture* and the cultural needs of diverse students.

School leaders who are in the position of evaluating the effectiveness of teachers need to be sure not to default to their own cultural expectations, but rather consider ways of communicating and supporting students that vary from their own cultural norms. Lisa Delpit's article, "The Silenced Dialogue: Power and Pedagogy in Educating Other People's Children" (1988), provides a rich source of insight about the ways in which different cultural modes of communication and pedagogy can affect the success of students in the classroom.

CHAPTER SUMMARY

Working on equity and inclusive education issues with teachers, secretaries, caretaking staff, educational assistants, and all other staff who are part of the school community requires strategies to facilitate deep personal reflection, honest dialogue, and collective commitment in a safe environment. It is important to set norms of operation and parameters for having courageous conversations. In this chapter we provided some ideas to act as catalysts for these discussions, such as personal stories, film clips, and analyzing barriers to inclusion. We also provided some starting points for working with teachers on addressing overt acts of harassment, practicing culturally relevant and responsive pedagogy, and engaging in personal action research. Finally, we raised some issues about the process of engaging in teacher supervision in culturally sensitive and equitable ways.

Case Study: "Stuck" in the Library

You are currently in a new assignment at a public school with a very diverse community. You quickly observe that the resources and decor in the library are not reflective of the students in the school. In reviewing teachers' annual learning plans (ALPs), you note that the teacher librarian has made no mention of building library resources that reflect the diversity of your school community. You have had several conversations with the teacher librarian about the importance of supporting and promoting equity and inclusive education in the school. She has been the teacher librarian at the school for 15 years, and she feels that she knows the students best, and she has already told you that you are the only principal that talks about this "equity thing." The library decor in winter and spring reflects Christmas and Easter, although the number of Christian families in the school is less than 10%. You value the experience she brings to the job and want her to continue in the role, but you know you must have a very important conversation with her about her ALP.

1. How will you approach this conversation? What would the conversation sound like?

2. How might you empower the librarian to pursue personal and professional growth in this area?

3. What supports might you offer to ensure both diversification of materials and promotion of their use?

4. What options will you consider should there be continued resistance to creating more equitable and inclusive practices in the resource center?

REFLECTION ACTIVITY: CRITICALLY QUESTIONING DAILY PRACTICES

In her discussion about addressing racial inequality and racism, Pollock (2008) suggests some questions to guide educators as they go about their work on a daily basis. These questions would also be helpful in keeping inquiry at play with respect to other areas of oppression, such as classism, homophobia, and gender inequities as well. She suggests the following questions:

- Am I seeing, understanding, and addressing the ways the world treats me and my students as race group members?
- Am I seeing, understanding, and addressing communities and individuals in their full complexity?
- Am I seeing, understanding, and addressing the ways opportunities to learn or thrive are unequally distributed to racial groups?

- What actions offer necessary opportunities to students in such a world?
- Do we think this action is moving students closer to a necessary educational opportunity, or farther away from it? Why? What is our evidence? (Pollock, 2008, pp. iii–iv)

Excerpt from *Everyday Antiracism: Getting Real About Race in School* © 2008 by Mica Pollock. Reprinted by permission of The new Press. www.thenewpress.com.

PRINCIPALS' ACTION STEPS

SELF

Reflect upon the degree to which staff see themselves and act as advocates for students and their families from an equity perspective. What might you do to further model a commitment to pervading life in the school with an equity focus?

OTHERS

View the video *Equity Frameworks* (Ontario Principals' Council, 2010) at http://www.prin cipals.ca/Display.aspx?cid=8194&pid=8075 with the administrative team and/or school improvement team and/or staff. This video will review some frameworks for engaging in personal reflection, dialogue, and action. Respond as a group to the Reflective Questions accompanying the video. As a supplement, view *Critical Issues Part 2: The Need for Action* as a catalyst for discussing further action plans.

TRY TOMORROW

Use Senge's Conversation Continuum, described in the *Equity Frameworks* video, to analyze and plan how conversations among staff might be moved along the continuum. See the Tools and Resources Section for a blackline master for this activity.

CHAPTER SIX

Working With Students

The world is moving on without me. I want to be turning with the world . . . not standing still. Stop the world. I want to get on.

Student who participated in a study
about at-risk and dropout students
(Toronto District School Board, 2005)

Our students are raising their voices. They are shouting to be heard. Listen again to Stephanie's *cri de coeur.* Reread the students' poem in the opening chapter. They want to be fully included, and they want to bring their full selves with them to school every day and to tell their stories. The late Theodore (Ted) Sizer was instrumental in shaping the educational and leadership philosophies of many administrators and teachers who were serious about school reform, particularly in the era following the Reagan administration's report *A Nation at Risk: The Imperative for Educational Reform* (National Commission on Excellence in Education, 1983). Sizer conducted a five-year study of high schools in which a team of investigators toured schools of various kinds, types, and locations; interviewed teachers, students, and administrators; and spent considerable time observing classrooms and, especially, following students through their daily routines. This study produced the Horace Trilogy—*Horace's Compromise* (1984), *Horace's School* (1992), and *Horace's Hope* (1996). Horace Smith, age 59, Sizer's archetype teacher, is considered a star staff member in the English department at Franklin High, a school of 1,350 students in the inner suburbs. Horace realizes that he does not know his kids well enough to really understand "how their minds work . . . [and] what motivates them. . . . But does he know them well enough to teach them powerfully, know the ways of their minds and moods? No, not even close" (Sizer, 1984, p. 4). So Horace compromises. He teaches those kids who make themselves interesting to him. The kids compromise, too. They reward their teachers by compromising. Each constituency understands the stakes. All know who the losers will be in this game.

In the second book in the trilogy, there are four questions that Sizer/Horace asks us to consider and address, in order and in combination. He and we believe them to be essential questions, and they are critical sites for reflection and action as we engage and work with students.

1. What is it that admirable high school graduates must display to deserve our respect and appreciation as well as their high school diploma?

2. How can schools function so that all adolescents have a fair chance to display these accomplishments? How can schools see to it that the maximum number of youngsters in fact achieves them?

3. What sort of political, administrative, and community context is required for schools that graduate such admirable young people?

4. How can the distinctive concerns of individual students, their families, the communities in which they reside, and the larger state be respectfully accommodated and yet still nurture schools and a schooling system that serves all adolescents?

Source: Sizer (1992, pp. 12–13).

These questions make it abundantly clear that the focus and emphasis must be on the students. What is it that we want them to do with their minds and hearts? That first question insists that we clarify both the destination and the means to reach the destination. This way of looking at the issue is not dissimilar from Ryan's (2006) view of leadership with its two essential components—"inclusive both in its nature and the ends for which it strives." Inclusive school leaders must therefore empower all students for lifelong learning by creating more inclusive environments and programs in schools and school communities. The means, therefore, must provide spaces for awakening the capacity for self-knowledge and self-expression. How do school leaders and teachers provide these spaces in both curricular and cocurricular settings? How do we work with students to involve them in schools that promote equity and social justice? These are the questions that will be explored in this chapter.

INCLUSIVE CURRICULUM

We return to curriculum and the definitions of inclusive curriculum that were previously mentioned as the starting points for assisting students such as Stephanie to "come to voice." Over and over again, we have pointed out that our students are not a monolithic group. They have complex social, cultural, and political lives with which we need to become familiar. Gaining a deeper knowledge and understanding of who our students and communities are will direct us toward developing more inclusive spaces and models for their learning. It is critical for staff to work toward creating an inclusive curriculum that represents the unique differences of every student in the classroom.

As we have demonstrated, James Banks's approaches to transforming the mainstream curriculum provide a thorough framework for what constitutes inclusive curriculum. We presented examples of making curriculum more inclusive so that all students see themselves reflected in the curriculum. Level 3, the Transformation Approach, for example, certainly addresses the majority of Sizer's essential questions. It changes instructional materials, teaching strategies, and student learning. It decenters the existing curriculum by bringing content about currently marginalized groups to the center of the curriculum.

> It helps students understand that how people construct knowledge depends on their experiences, values, and perspectives. It helps students learn to construct knowledge themselves. And it helps students grasp the complex group interactions that have produced the American culture and civilization. (Banks, 1994, p. 6)

Focusing on curriculum in all its aspects—content, pedagogy, access, and climate—must become the obsession of all school leaders in working with students.

THE MIRRORS AND WINDOWS CONCEPT

> *If the student is understood as occupying a dwelling of self, education needs to enable the student to look through window frames in order to see the realities of others and into mirrors in order to see her/his own reality reflected.*

(Style, 1996, p. 35)

Christine Sleeter has expanded on this metaphor in the development of her multicultural frameworks. She explains that students who belong to a dominant culture "experience curriculum as a mirror." Although they may be introduced to new concepts and develop new skills, the curriculum is

> still anchored in a worldview that they have grown up with, and peopled with figures that are roughly like them. The opposite is usually true of students from non-dominant groups, who experience curriculum mainly as a window into the dominant society's world. (Sleeter as quoted in Mishra, 2011, para. 1)

Reflecting on these remarks in the light of Sizer's essential questions and reflecting on my own personal experience, I recall that it took several endings and beginnings for me to find the right graduate school and program that would provide me with both mirrors and windows. Far too many of our students have comparable experiences in high school, which can result in disinterest, disengagement, and dropouts. The Style/Sleeter approach acknowledges the importance of students seeing themselves and their experiences reflected in classroom resources—"eyesight and insight"—while at the same time honoring the notion that students benefit from broadening their horizons through exposure to perspectives and experiences that are different from their own. Further, exposure to books and media that reflect what might on the surface appear to reflect different cultural experiences can also lead to finding the emotions and sensibilities that connect us as human beings.

However, Sleeter (2008) cautions that "adjusting curriculum to offer students both mirrors and windows is tricky because it is easy to make inaccurate and stereotypical assumptions. First, it is dangerous to assume that, by looking at students and reading their names, [we] can accurately identify their racial backgrounds" (p. 151). This approach acknowledges the fact "that sometimes students would be drawn to material reflecting people like themselves while at other times they would want to read about someone different from themselves" (p. 152).

STUDENT LEADERSHIP AND VOICE

When looking at issues of student engagement, one of the important factors to be addressed is student leadership. Students need to take responsibility, and when they do, they have a greater stake in the outcome. Students need to be given opportunities to be equitable partners in their education. In order to achieve equity for students, this component of student engagement must be in place.

Generally speaking, students find it easier to discuss and deal with issues of inequity and oppression, such as racism, than adults do (Pollock, 2008). Finding ways to include students in the decision making and equity work in the school and beyond provides powerful potential for creating a more inclusive environment. One of the most powerful ways we can encourage students to take equity seriously is to model and promote it in our attitudes, actions, and behaviors. The story in Chapter 1 of the vice principal who provides the charge for educating the school community about how to combat homophobia is an excellent example. It is also an excellent demonstration of students, staff, and parents coming to voice to become agents of change.

Ryan (2006) describes three good reasons for providing students with leadership opportunities. The first is that we acknowledge the rights of students, as described in the United Nations' *Convention on the Rights of the Child* (General Assembly of the United Nations, 1989/1990) to have a voice and the participatory rights of a citizen in processes that affect their wellbeing. Second, the chance to use their extensive knowledge of life in the classroom and in schools cannot help but improve their engagement and motivation to make a difference. They know far more about incidents that take place beyond the gaze of the adults in the building, and about practices that alienate and marginalize both students and families, as we have shared in Chapter 4 through the research conducted by William Preble and others. They also have a vital role to play in holding the system's feet to the fire when the promise of policy does not translate into practice and does not change the realities of the student experience. Finally, students learn about democratic processes best by being involved in them, rather than merely studying about them in the abstract. In Ryan's view, students should be included as leaders for both "moral and pragmatic reasons" (2006, p. 82).

SOCIAL JUSTICE INITIATIVES

Among social justice researchers, there are very few individuals who are not familiar with Peggy McIntosh's *White Privilege: Unpacking the Invisible Knapsack* (1988), which was responsible for introducing generations of readers to a deeper understanding of the concepts of unearned power and privilege. Martin Haberman's article "The Pedagogy of Poverty Versus Good Teaching" (2005) struck a similar chord by drawing a clear distinction between a limited set of behaviors commonly regarded as acts of teaching in urban schools and good teaching behaviors, which tend to be evident more in what the students are doing than in the observable actions of the teacher. In the latter, the student is the active/activist learner, and the teacher is the facilitator of learning opportunities. Haberman's view is in striking alignment with Level 4—the Social Action Approach—of the James Banks framework. This approach calls for students to acquire the knowledge and commitment needed to think, decide, and take personal, social, and civic action. In his article, "Transforming the Mainstream Curriculum" (1994), Banks quotes Clegg: "Activism helps students apply what they have learned and develop a sense of personal and civic efficacy."

Compare this to what is written on an immense sign that Haberman saw hanging in a high school that has devoted itself to raising test scores: "We dispense knowledge. Bring your own container." Instead of filling the pail, we should be lighting the fire. It is important to have students working on local and global social justice issues. Students need to see the work outside of themselves and their immediate circle of influence. In order for students to become more equitable themselves, they need to be given responsibilities around social justice for others. Leaders within the school must provide students with opportunities to be involved in social justice work both locally and, eventually, globally. If this is achieved for students and they participate in social justice activities, then they will be on the road to becoming champions of equity and social justice.

Many years ago, the school cafeteria in one our schools was a filthy mess of dirty tables, with uneaten food scraps left on tables and floors, wet paper napkins clinging to all surfaces, and so on waiting for the caretaking/janitorial staff to clean up. Public requests, teacher chats, and administrators' pleas fell on deaf ears. Then a group of senior students took action and formed a group named the Pig Pen Patrol and began to supervise their peers and motivate them to change behaviors—this was a successful strategy that worked!!!

One way to provide students with opportunities to be involved in social justice work is to encourage the formation of extracurricular groups for this purpose. Some activities for such groups are suggested in Table 6.1.

STUDENT ACTION RESEARCH

Action research about issues of equity conducted by students, and presented to peers, teachers, staff, and community, is a powerful tool for heightening awareness and creating a call for action. In one school, for example, a teacher committed to issues of equity involved Grade 6 to 8 students in group projects that investigated social issues both in the school and in the local community. One group, after studying issues related to homelessness, videotaped interviews conducted in a local shelter. In partnership with the interviewees, they captured the complexity and poignancy of the issues related to homelessness. They not only shared the resulting video with the school community but also submitted it to the City Student Film

Table 6.1   Suggested Activities for Equity and Social Justice Groups/Clubs

Elementary	*Secondary*
Establishing a Social Justice Club • Students will develop a rationale for a club, show how it relates to curriculum and school improvement, and seek a staff advisor. • Students will develop an advertisement for the school newspaper/website/weekly bulletin to describe the club, its mission/vision, activities, et cetera. • Students will develop a poster that will attract members to join the club. • Students will use the public address system in the school to make announcements about the initiative. • Students will visit classrooms to publicize and gain support for this initiative. • Each of these media requires a different style of communication and a different register of language.	**Mirrors and Windows Activity** • Education needs to enable us to look through *window* frames to see the realities of others and into *mirrors* to see our own reality. • Education engages us in *"the great conversation"* between various frames of reference. **Think/Pair/Share Activity** • *Think* of a book, picture, play, story, poem, novel, movie, video, lecture, experience, or something similar that had/has strong appeal for you. • *Pair* conversation—discuss with a partner: Why did you make this choice? What do you find in this work that serves as a window to another way of living/being that is strange and unfamiliar to you? What do you find in this work that serves as a mirror of your own life, reflecting something familiar that you can easily recognize? • *Share* conversation—discuss with class: In what ways do you think the character(s) or social actor(s) live(s) a different life from yours? Different values, needs, hopes, expectations? In what ways do you think the character(s) or social actor(s) is/are like you? Similar values? What else? How can you use this activity as "inspiration" and "perspiration" for your social justice work?

Festival, where they won first prize, therefore widening even further their sphere of influence. Their project also was a catalyst for the student body to "adopt" the local shelter for initiatives such as collecting and providing warm winter wear.

A second group designed a project to investigate the attitudes of students toward different racialized groups and toward gay/lesbian populations. Their video, shared with other classes, staff, and the school council, provided rich data for establishing the need to actively and deliberately promote more inclusive attitudes. When audiences could see before their very eyes the data that were collected in their own school, it was not an option to remain silent and fail to act.

HONORING NONCURRICULAR SKILLS AND CONTRIBUTIONS

Another important, yet often overlooked, issue in working equitably with students is the need to honor skills that are significant accomplishments not recognized by mainstream curriculum and assessment. These might include the ability to speak multiple languages, to translate/interpret into other languages, or to balance extensive home and school responsibilities. Hamann (2008) cites the example of students who are often called upon by teachers to act as translators/interpreters in order to facilitate communication with new students or with family/community members. This is an area of skill that demonstrates high levels of ability and provides significant service, and yet because it is not itemized as an area of achievement in mainstream curricula, these accomplishments remain unrecognized in a formal way. Finding ways to highlight these abilities within our current standards-based approach to education, such as by anecdotally recording them on report cards and/ or including certificates of commendation in their formal student record files, would at least begin to rectify this failure to honor nonstandard accomplishments. In the long run, of course, continuing to question and speak up against a standards-based focus that favors the needs and interests of the dominant group will need to be a priority if we are to find a way to educate all of our students in a just and equitable way.

CHAPTER SUMMARY

In this chapter, we looked at students as the focus for equitable practice in our schools using a two-fold approach: How do school leaders provide space for all students to flourish in equitable ways? How do we elicit students' voices and involve them in working toward socially just ends? We looked first at inclusive curriculum, using the James Banks framework to consider content, pedagogy, access, and climate. We then considered the "mirrors and windows" model (Style, 1996) for providing curricular resources that both reflect the experiences of our diverse students and provide them with opportunities to see and understand the perspectives of others. Next, we discussed the moral and pragmatic reasons for fostering student leadership and voice, followed by ideas for engaging students in social justice initiatives, such as student action research. Finally we considered the importance of formally honoring the diverse student skills and contributions that are not valued in our current standards-based approach to curriculum and achievement.

Case Study: What's It All About?

Central High School has recently celebrated its 75th anniversary. The school is located in a neighborhood that has become increasingly racially and ethnically diverse over the years. Students come from both sides of the tracks, literally and figuratively. To the south of the school district are expensive upper middle class homes, and these parents no longer view the school as a preferred site for schooling for their kids. They find ways to send their kids to alternative school sites out of the area or to private schools. The students who come from north of the school live in public housing. Their parents are strong supporters of the school.

You are the new principal and you have been invited to the first meeting of this year's prom committee. The committee is composed of a group of beautiful blonde girls of European descent who demonstrate a clear certainty about the prom's location, meal, and music and the evening's activities, which include crowning a king and queen. The conversation reminds you of a meeting with members of the yearbook committee, where you had pushed back at the students' desire to include categories/photographs of the year's student prince and student princess. The students were not pleased at your request for discarding the idea and adopting a more inclusive approach. Apparently, the teacher who is the yearbook advisor is supportive of the idea.

1. How do you proceed in both the short term and long term in getting the players to shift positions/interests?

2. How do you use the concept of mirrors and windows to assist you in your deliberations and actions?

REFLECTION ACTIVITY

The following figure highlights types of activities for engaging students in questioning, understanding, and contributing in tangible ways to social justice issues and pursuits. Engage your staff and student representatives in a conversation about those that are currently offered and those that might be developed in order to foster greater student voice and leadership.

Students enjoy projects that involve them in

- activities that meet their needs and interests.
- activities that empower them as leaders.
- issues that they regard as vital concerns, for example, school dress code, censorship in the school newspaper, student morale, et cetera.
- explanations of human differences, for example, homelessness, the disabled, poverty, gender equality, global public health, infant mortality, et cetera.
- seeing big ideas, major concepts, and global dilemmas.
- planning, action research, and analysis.
- debating global issues, for example, war, health care, child labor, global warming, world hunger, environmental sustainability, et cetera.
- first-hand experiences, real-life experiences.
- information technology, social media.
- community service, service learning.
- telling their own stories.

PRINCIPALS' ACTION STEPS

SELF   Your underserved students are shouting:
                        "Stop the world. I want to get on." In three
                        sentences, how can you reassure them that
                        you have heard them?

OTHERS   Share your response with your staff. View
                        the video *Closing the Achievement Gap*
                        (Ontario Principals' Council, 2010) at http://
                        www.principals.ca/Display.aspx?cid=8194
                        &pid=8075. Respond as a group to the Reflec-
                        tive Questions accompanying the video.

TRY TOMORROW   How might you start to get to know one of
                        the underserved students whose voice you
                        heard?

CHAPTER SEVEN

Working With Community

*The nation's schools must improve education for all chil-
dren, but schools cannot do this alone. More will be
accomplished if schools, families, and communities work
together to promote successful students.*

(Epstein, n.d.)

WHAT IS A FAMILY?

In the opening chapter, we described school as a place where
students come with their embodiments of race, sex, gender, socioeconomic class, and ability/disability. They also come with more—
their families.

> Families come with their children to school. Even when they do
> not come in person, families come in children's minds and
> hearts and in their hopes and dreams. They come with the
> children's problems and promise. Without exception, teachers
> and administrators have explicit or implicit contact with their
> students' families every day. (Epstein, 2011, p. 4)

Do we know the names, the faces, the stories of our students'
parents and families? Do we truly recognize families in all their
diversity? There are still so many prevailing assumptions about

what constitutes a family. What is a family? One of my principal colleagues recently revealed that it took him many years before he felt comfortable about displaying a photograph of his family on his desk. His family consists of his male partner and their two young adopted sons who are of different ethnicities from their parents. So it is part of the principal's responsibility to work with teachers to broaden their collective understanding and appreciation for the vast number of family structures that are a part of their school communities. A helpful tool for this process is the multiple-award-winning short documentary, *That's a Family,* available on YouTube:

That's a Family
http://www.youtube.com/watch?v=lnYWCtX3Us4

SCHOOL, FAMILY, AND COMMUNITY PARTNERSHIPS

If schools are developing and delivering programs and learning opportunities for students and their diverse families each and every day, how do we all come together to share responsibility for student success? What methods, processes, and resources will yield success for students and their families and communities?

Epstein et al. (2002) identify six types of involvement for successful school–family–community partnerships and the possible outcomes for student success (Figure 7.1).

For more comprehensive information on the National Network of Partnership Schools Partnership Model, please visit http://www .csos.jhu.edu/p2000/program.htm.

Some ministries and departments of education have come to appreciate and understand the benefits of school, family, and community partnerships for school improvement and closing the achievement gap, as evidenced by the Ontario Ministry of Education's insertion of the Parent Engagement Office within its Equity and Inclusive Education Branch. In 2010, Ontario produced *Parents in Partnership: A Parent Engagement Policy for*

Figure 7.1   The Keys to Successful School–Family–Community
Partnerships

The keys to successful
school-family-community partnerships
Epstein's six types of involvement

PARENTING: Assist families in understanding child and adolescent development, and in setting home conditions that support children as students at each age and grade level. Assist schools in understanding families.

COMMUNICATING: Communicate with families about school programs and student progress through effective school-to-home and home-to-school communications.

VOLUNTEERING: Improve recruitment, training, work, and schedules to involve families as volunteers and audiences at school or in other locations to support students and school programs.

LEARNING AT HOME: Involve families with their children in learning activities at home, including homework, other curriculum-related activities, and individual course and program decisions.

DECISION MAKING: Include families as participants in school decisions, governance, and advocacy through School Council, committees, action teams, and other parent organizations.

COLLABORATING WITH COMMUNITY: Coordinate resources and services for students, families, and the school with businesses, agencies, and other groups, and provide services to the community.

(Continued)

Figure 7.1 (Continued)

Possible Outcomes for Student Success
Studies show that each type of
involvement promotes *different* kinds of results.

Type 1 – Parenting	→	Students improve when families are provided information on child development and school expectations at each grade level (e.g., to support student health, behavior, attendance).
Type 2 – Communicating	→	Students increase awareness of their own progress in subjects and skills when teachers, students, and parents communicate about classwork.
Type 3 – Volunteering	→	Students gain academic skills that are tutored or taught by volunteers.
Type 4 – Learning at Home	→	Students complete more homework in specific subjects when teachers guide parents in how to interact on assignments.
Type 5 – Decision Making	→	Students benefit from policies and projects conducted and supported by parent organizations and partnership teams.
Type 6 – Collaborating with the Community	→	Students gain skills and talents in curricular, extra-curricular, and afterschool projects with community partners.

Each Type of Involvement Also Can Strengthen Specific Results →

Source: From *School, Family, and Community Partnerships: Your Handbook for Action*, 2nd ed., by J. L. Epstein et al., 2002, Thousand Oaks, CA: Corwin. Reprinted with permission.

Ontario Schools. This policy fulfills the ministry's commitment to support and enhance parent engagement by

- articulating a vision of parent engagement in Ontario schools.
- identifying the strategies necessary to fulfill the vision of parent engagement and support Ontario's core priorities for education.
- identifying and removing discriminatory biases and systemic barriers in order to allow participation of all parents in their children's schools, with the goal of supporting student learning and helping to close the achievement gap.
- promoting specific parent involvement practices that are known to positively influence student learning and achievement.
- identifying the roles of education partners—including the ministry, school boards, schools, parent involvement committees, and school councils—in furthering parent engagement across the province.

Source: Ontario Ministry of Education (2010).

In this chapter, we will use these core beliefs and actions to engage school leaders in a conversation about the development, maintenance, and expansion of partnerships with diverse communities that support school improvement so that the perspectives and experiences of all students, families, and employees are recognized and their needs are met.

ARTICULATING A VISION FOR PARENT ENGAGEMENT

The term *parent engagement* has been part of the language of public education for decades. The implication has been that we're doing it or we've already done it, so let's put a check mark in that box and move on to more critical paths to student learning. However, in the schools of the 21st century, what do we really mean by parent engagement, and even more important, why is parent engagement necessary for fostering a climate of equity and inclusion within a school? For the purposes of this book and as we have talked about in Chapter 4 on school climate, parent engagement goes well beyond parents attending concerts, sports days, interviews, and social events at the school.

The title of Ontario's parent engagement policy—*Parents in Partnership*—provides an excellent starting point for reflecting on a vision for family and community involvement in schools. The word *partner* introduces notions of a shared vision, purpose, and ownership. It also resonates with tones of respect and trust—concepts that are not always easy to make tangible. That was certainly the case in the events in one school district that resulted in a total school administrative reorganization when Black and Hispanic parents in a very diverse community felt that they were being marginalized and excluded from formal roles on the school council on the basis of socioeconomic class. These parents told stories of the former administration "speaking down" to them while being welcoming and invitational to white middle class parents—a sharp reminder of the importance of using a language of inclusivity, a language of dialogue, in communicating with our school communities.

> Dialogue is oriented toward inquiry for the purpose of developing a collective understanding of a given topic. Dialogue attempts to bridge the perceived or real differences among speakers. . . . Participants seek to understand others' viewpoints and experiences and the underlying reasons for others' thoughts and actions, and participants reflect on their own viewpoints and experiences. Thus, participants in dialogue gain information and insight not only about others but also about themselves. (Lindsey et al., p. 136)

Henderson et al. (2007, p. 14) pose a powerful question: "What might a school look like that has created a genuine culture of school–family–community partnership, and that has made real progress toward high social and academic achievement for all students?" They go on to offer four levels of descriptors to determine actual progress:

Partnership School	All families and communities have something great to offer—we do whatever it takes to work closely together to make sure every single student succeeds.
Open-Door School	Parents can be involved in our school in many ways—we're working hard to get an even bigger turnout for our activities. When we ask the community to help, people often respond.

Come-If-We-Call School	Parents are welcome when we ask them, but there's only so much they can offer. The most important thing they can do is help their kids at home. We know where to get help in the community if we need it.
Fortress School	Parents belong at home, not at school. If students don't do well, it's because their families don't give them enough support. We're already doing all we can. Our school is an oasis in a troubled community. We want to keep it that way.

Source: Henderson et al. (2007, pp. 14–18).

In addition to the above descriptions, Henderson et al. provide a rubric with opportunities to reflect on the following areas: building relationships, linking to learning, addressing differences, supporting advocacy, and sharing power. There are also a number of checklists on the areas mentioned that take the reader from a place of "already doing this" through "could do this easily," and "this will take time" to "this will be hard." Where does your school fall within the rubric?

Reflecting on the questions in the box below will help to prepare your school to establish constructive partnerships.

Reflect on These Questions in Preparation for Establishing Constructive Partnerships

- What would be some quick routes to pursue?

_____

_____

_____

- What needs a more deliberate stance?

_____

_____

_____

(Continued)

(Continued)

- What are your core beliefs about family and community engagement?

_____

_____

_____

- How are they integrated into your school's mission/vision?

_____

_____

_____

- Are all families welcomed, respected, and valued as partners in their children's learning and development? In what ways?

_____

_____

_____

- Do all families have opportunities to be involved? In what ways?

_____

_____

_____

- Do they have a full range of choices about how to be involved to support student success? Describe these choices.

_____

_____

_____

- Are all parents engaged through ongoing communication and dialogue with other educational partners to support a positive learning environment at home and at school? In what ways?

_____

_____

_____

- Are all parents supported with the information and tools necessary to participate in school life?

  _____

  _____

  _____

A viable vision of parent and community engagement needs to see families as true partners in education who are directly involved in helping to create and deliver the school's curriculum. If you are committed to community partnerships, then it is important to also be committed to equity. You cannot authentically include and value the distinctive concerns and viewpoints of diverse communities unless you are committed to looking at issues through an equity lens. It means stepping out of your own comfort zone and allowing others' opinions to be valued and included. Developing and implementing school plans for improved student achievement requires the activation of the knowledge(s), skills, and talents of all members of the entire school community, and it is in the hands of school leaders to ignite the process.

GETTING TO KNOW YOUR COMMUNITY

Teachers usually take the first month of the school year really getting to know who their students are. They consider the students' interests and their strengths, motivations, and areas for growth. You may recall how Sizer's archetypal teacher, Horace, mentioned in Chapter 6, struggled to uncover the authentic identities in his classroom. It should be no different when looking at community from the role of the principal. Getting to know your community is an essential part of a school leader's entry plan. It starts with your core beliefs, which are the foundation of all your attitudes and behaviors. It is not enough to meet and greet parents and welcome them to the school. It is also not enough to have posters on the walls that portray students' communities.

To truly get to know your school community means taking the time to dialogue with community members about what they value and what they see as important when it comes to education. What are their beliefs and values? It also means understanding their religious and cultural values and looking at ways to incorporate these into your school's culture. Getting to know your community can take many forms—both informal and formal. It may mean taking the time to have a conversation with parents when they drop off or pick up their children or when they come into the school to see a teacher. It may mean going out to the local mall and meeting the parents in the community. It may take more formal means through focused group conversations with various parents, school council meetings, parent-teacher conferences, and curriculum focused information sessions. In order to get authentic engagement of the parent community, the principal must be open to including values and viewpoints from a diverse group of people. This becomes even more important when the principal's cultural values and beliefs may differ from those of the community she or he serves. This takes us back to earlier chapters, where we discussed the importance of the personal journey of educational leaders in order to work toward equity, diversity, and inclusivity. Principals must reflect on their own stereotypes and biases and unpack their own assumptions and beliefs, which may impact how they view the curriculum, the students, and the community.

BUILDING COMMUNICATION

Working with teachers to build bridges to span the cultural disconnect that is often experienced by many members of the school community is key to creating more inclusive relationships. In describing the impetus for beginning their "Colorful Flags" program, designed to address the "bubble of mistrust" that can sometimes exist among individuals who have had different cultural experiences, Reese (2001) recounts the following anecdote:

An incident that happened to me as I was implementing the Colorful Flags program in the schools showed me the value of my new approach to overcoming the original state of ethnic relations. One day in the summer of 1994, I went to pick up my car at a repair shop in South-Central Los Angeles. I asked the mechanic, an elderly Korean–American gentleman, if he had serviced my muffler. "Yes" the mechanic said. I asked him if he had serviced my transmission. "Yes" the mechanic said. The next thing I said to this gentleman brought tears to his eyes. I looked him in the eyes, I put my hand out, and I said, "Comop sin me dah," which is "thank you" in Korean. At first his mouth dropped, and then his eyes watered. He had never heard an American, let alone an African American, attempt to speak his language. It was not my perfect pronunciation that brought tears to the gentleman's eyes, nor was it my perfect syntax or grammar. It was the attempt. It was the effort of trying to reach out to him, to show him I cared about him and his culture, through the most intimate vehicle we know, which is language. (2001, "The Colorful Flags Program," para. 1)

In response to this experience, Reese (2001) proposed a program based on a "proactive-interactive human relations approach" to encourage others to learn basic words and phrases to connect with and honor the languages of others with whom he works. His argument is that these simple acts send powerful messages to others that they are worthy and respected in our eyes. After all, most people do this naturally when they travel to a place with a dominant language other than their own. Why not make it a priority to do it in our own school and community contexts? For teachers, resources abound for learning the basic phrases for communicating simple messages such as "hello," "how are you?" and "thank you." Students can be involved with you in composing charts such as the ones below and posting them in classrooms and hallways for easy reference for all in the school.

Language	Hello	Goodbye	How are you?	Thank you
Spanish				
Somali				
Mandarin				
Hindi				

Beginning to engage in an activity such as this creates a self-perpetuating flow of good will, empowering both self and others.

Additional Concrete Strategies for Getting to Know Your Community

- Hold staff meetings periodically in community venues, with presentations from community members.
- Balance "curriculum nights"—where school staff present information about the school and the curriculum to the community, with "community nights"—where community members and staff have an opportunity to get to know each other, so that the flow of information/teaching/learning flows in both directions.

CAPACITY BUILDING FOR FAMILY AND COMMUNITY ENGAGEMENT AND PARTNERSHIPS

Often, parent engagement is measured by the number of parents who attend your seasonal concert or school-based extracurricular activities. We are suggesting that you look at parent engagement through a more inclusive lens. Parent engagement means parents need to be involved in their children's education, which includes curriculum development and delivery. It is important to build capacity in parents by educating them about the curriculum and the role they may wish to play in developing it. In one school with a very high immigrant population, workshops were set up for parents on the different areas of the curriculum and how they were being taught. This not only allowed parents to increase their understanding of the education system, but it also allowed them to be involved in the creation of the curriculum and to help their children at home. These examples are excellent demonstrations of Epstein's Type 1–Parenting and Type 4–Learning at Home forms of involvement.

This approach to capacity building with parents is critical if parents are going to be authentically involved in their children's education. This can lead to deeper involvement instead of the quantitative kind of surface involvement that is often measured by the school administration. When you build this capacity, parents' trust and confidence levels increase, and they will ask new questions and seek further clarification. However we do need to be mindful that not all parents will take these opportunities for capacity building and not judge those parents who cannot or do not wish to attend parent workshops. Epstein reminds us that we need to redefine certain kinds of family involvement. The family workshop is not about attendance; the workshop is the content of the meeting. We need to find a variety of ways to get the information out—Type 3–Communicating—by summarizing it on paper or through telephone messaging, video, the school's website, or some other form of communication.

Earlier we introduced the notion of intentionality in terms of ensuring that principles of equity and inclusive education permeate all aspects of system and school policies and practices. We need to bring this same spirit of intentionality into planning for family and community engagement. The principal alone cannot create an enduring, comprehensive program that involves all families as their children progress through all grades. Parent engagement does not stop at the end of elementary school; it continues right through to Grade 12.

Who works to create these lasting partnerships? Epstein (2011), who has designed the six types of involvement, suggests a five-step approach to capacity building. She recommends that the school improvement team and the school council create at plan for partnerships each year and a team to implement it.

All schools should use an action team for partnerships (ATP) "to organize and sustain a program of school, family, and community partnerships." The ATP should include the principal, teachers from different grade levels, parents with children at different grade levels, students from different grade levels, members of the community at large, and school support employees.

The plan should include the specific activities that the ATP will implement, improve, or maintain; a timeline of monthly actions needed for each activity; a list of who is responsible for each activity (both ATP members and others); a means of evaluating each activity; and any other details of importance.

The five steps are as follows:

STEP 1	Create an action team for partnerships (ATP).	The ATP is an "action arm" of a school council or school improvement team. The ATP takes responsibility for assessing existing partnership practices, organizing options for new partnerships, implementing selected activities, delegating responsibilities, evaluating progress, and planning next steps.

(Continued)

(Continued)

STEP 2	Obtain funds and other support.	A modest budget is needed to guide and support the activities planned by the ATP. The ATP must have sufficient time and support to plan and evaluate activities and time to conduct the activities in the annual plan for partnerships.
STEP 3	Identify starting points.	The ATP takes stock of existing practices: present strengths, needed changes, expectations, sense of community, and links to goals.
STEP 4	Develop a one-year action plan.	The detailed plan will address details, responsibilities, costs, and evaluation and will be shared with the school council, school improvement team, parent organization, and all teachers, parents, and students.
STEP 5	Continue planning, evaluating, and improving programs.	The ATP should schedule an annual presentation and celebration of progress with the school community and gather input from all to develop a new and improved one-year action plan for partnerships.

You will find a complete presentation of this framework in Dr. Joyce L. Epstein's *School, Family, and Community Partnerships: Preparing Educators and Improving Schools* (2011) and also in *School, Family, and Community Partnerships: Your Handbook for Action* (2002).

You will also find useful strategies that encourage and support intentionality in the previously cited *Beyond the Bake Sale: The Essential Guide to Family-School Partnerships* (Henderson et al., 2007). In Section III of this book, "Guidelines for Action From Research," the authors explore in great detail—with accompanying scoring sheets and checklists related to their areas of research—the levels of achievement that were described earlier:

- Linking to Learning: How Will Involving Parents Help Your Test Scores?
- Addressing Differences: How Can You Deal with Issues of Race, Class, and Culture?

- Supporting Advocacy: How Can "Problem Parents" Become Partners You Can Work With?
- Sharing Power: Who's in Charge Here Anyway?
- Scaling Up: Why Can't All Schools in a District Create Strong Partnerships with Families? (Henderson et al., 2007)

These are all approaches that ensure that we promote family and community involvement practices that are known to positively influence student learning and achievement. These approaches are also directly linked to all five areas of the leader practices and competencies listed in Ontario's *Leadership Framework for Principals and Vice-Principals*—Setting Directions, Building Relationships and Developing People, Developing the Organization, Leading the Instructional Program, and Securing Accountability (http://www.edu.gov.on.ca/eng/policyfunding/leadership/PVPLeadership Framework.pdf).

REDUCING AND ELIMINATING BARRIERS

barrier: An obstacle to equity that may be overt or subtle, intended or unintended, and systemic or specific to an individual or group, and that prevents or limits access to opportunities, benefits, or advantages that are available to other members of society.

(Ontario Ministry of Education, 2009a)

In Chapter 2, we examined the concepts of power and privilege and showed how they marginalized and excluded numerous voices from critical conversations on school improvement. In the narrative that opens Chapter 4, we presented an example of a "fortress school" with a visible, physical, concrete barrier in the office that kept the community out. Equitable and inclusive schools seek to understand, identify, address, and eliminate biases, barriers, and power dynamics that limit many students' and communities' access to opportunities in the system and to full participatory school–community relations. Barriers may be related to gender, race, ethnicity, religion, class, physical or mental ability, sexual orientation, and/or other factors. Since there is also the probability that several other factors may intersect to create additional barriers, school leaders and school teams must develop and offer a smorgasbord of strategies that facilitate inclusivity.

Are there child care issues? Can students in the neighboring secondary schools assist? In one particular school with a high immigrant population, many of the children were being raised by their mothers only because the fathers worked overseas to make ends meet. These mothers could not attend school council meetings or workshops for parents sponsored by the school, because they had no one to care for their children while they attended. The principal reduced this barrier by providing child care through the city's parks and recreation division, so that every mother who wanted to attend could do so knowing that their children would be taken care of. This same principal reduced the language gap by offering every workshop for parents in three different languages.

What about transportation? Many parents in inner-city schools do not have cars and live relatively far from the school. You may need to provide a bus or organize a car pool. In Ontario, the Ministry of Education's Parents Reaching Out grants program supports for school-based initiatives focused on engaging parents who may be experiencing barriers as a result of language, recent immigration, poverty, newcomer status, unfamiliarity with the system, or for other reasons. Schools can also reach out to communities by serving as resources to address community needs. During the summer of 2005, when our city was troubled by a wave of youth violence, the Focus on Youth and Community Use of Schools programs were instrumental in providing school spaces for communities to initiate programs for families and to keep students off the streets and engaged in purposeful activities.

CHAPTER SUMMARY

The centuries-old African proverb, "It takes a whole village to raise a child," is often quoted in education circles to describe a romanticized vision for the public education system and the larger society. We argue that schools must strive to truly become "partnership schools" where families and communities are equal partners in relationships that are built on trust and mutual respect. School teams must take an audit of their current circumstances, intentionally reach out to their communities, learn who their communities are, and consciously work with this knowledge to go beyond the limited traditional roles for families and community members. They must also create a positive school climate free from discriminatory barriers and develop an action plan for partnerships that creates a culture of learning and achievement, as well as strong supports for community members and broad and deep outreach to the entire school community.

Case Study: Trouble With Penguins

This morning, as part of her unit on families, one of the Grade 2 teachers reads the picture book *Tango Makes Three* to her students. The book is a delightful, true story about two male penguins in the Central Park Zoo in New York who find an abandoned egg, build a nest, keep the egg warm, and then nurture the newborn penguin until it is grown. The teacher's intent was to help her students realize and appreciate the fact that families can have many different structures.

This afternoon after school, you received a phone call from an angry parent who informed you that the next time the teacher read a book about homosexuality, she wanted to be informed and wanted her child removed from the classroom. You invited the parent to come to the school tomorrow morning to discuss the matter with you.

1. How might your conversation with this parent unfold?

2. What are the issues around human rights and valuing difference that might develop?

3. What will your response be to the parent's request?

REFLECTION ACTIVITY 1

In the previous chapter, we introduced the concept of windows and mirrors from the work of Style (1996) and Sleeter (2008, 2011). Now try the following activity, adapted from Dufour et al. (2004) and cited in *Beyond the Bake Sale: The Essential Guide to Family-School Partnerships* (Hendersonet al., 2007).

Ask your school staff, school improvement team, and/or action team for partnerships to brainstorm what would improve parent, family, and community involvement at your school. Put the ideas that shift the responsibility to people or sources outside the school (looking out the window) in one column and ideas that give responsibility to people or sources inside the school (looking in the mirror) in another. Do not label the columns; let the participants figure it out. Then talk about the contrast between the items in the two columns.

REFLECTION ACTIVITY 2

- Brainstorm to make a list of typical ways of engaging families in schools, e.g., "Meet the Teacher" Night, recruiting families as volunteers.
- Adopt one of the following five lenses. You are

  1. a recent female immigrant from Iran with limited facility in English.
  2. a father with a same sex partner. Your son has been harassed at school for having gay parents.
  3. a single white mother struggling with two low-income jobs and two young children.
  4. a First Nations/American Indian father who was educated on a reserve/reservation but now lives in the city. You work the night shift.
  5. a Black parent of two sons who have dropped out of school and whose last son is "at risk."

- Through this lens, review the brainstormed list, asking which activities might be difficult for you to access or to feel comfortable attending, and why.

How might these activities be modified to create greater inclusion in your school?

PRINCIPALS' ACTION STEPS

SELF   Reflect on how you show the community
                        who you really are outside of your prescribed

role. How do/can you use those outside passions/interests to connect more deeply with your school community?

OTHERS

View the video *Engaging Parents and Communities* (Ontario Principals' Council, 2010) at http://www.principals.ca/Display.aspx?cid=8194&pid=8075 with staff and community. Select some of the Reflective Questions that accompany the video for discussion.

TRY TOMORROW

Select one strategy that you will use to show students who you really are outside of your principal role. Use that strategy to show them that you value their home worlds.

CHAPTER EIGHT

Assessing Progress

> *The principal is responsible for creating conditions for student success and is accountable to students, parents, the community, supervisors, and to the board for ensuring that students benefit from a high quality education. The principal is specifically accountable for the goals set out in the school improvement plan.*
>
> (Institute for Education Leadership, 2008)

S uccessful implementation of school policies on equity and inclusive education depends on commitment, coordination, and cooperation from the entire school community. It is an individual school's responsibility to assess and report progress to the school district and community and to review and establish self-assessment processes to determine the effectiveness of the school's equity and inclusive education plans and procedures. In previous chapters, we have discussed the use of a variety of assessment tools, such as the Cultural Proficiency Continuum, to look at growth in culturally responsible beliefs and practices, and the James Banks framework to assess the depth and effectiveness of pedagogical response to diversity. In this chapter we will highlight one successful approach and accompanying framework—the Equity Walk—that could facilitate the principal's efforts to provide accountability and transparency in monitoring and reporting progress on school improvement. In suggesting the use of this, or any other, framework, we subscribe to the belief that the best assessment of a school community's growth in equity and inclusive education is a process co-created by the members of that community, based on its unique characteristics and needs. Therefore, any framework or model should be viewed as only a starting point, one that is malleable to suit the needs of the particular context.

EQUITY AND REFLECTIVE PRACTICE

In preparation for engaging with the "Equity Walk: A Research-Informed Practice," school leaders must incorporate leadership behaviors that go beyond a tolerance for diversity toward a transformation for equity. Lindsey et al. (2005) relate how a group of superintendents engaged in a series of three-hour sessions held at six-week intervals and developed three outcomes for their work:

- As educational leaders, they would view issues of cultural power to be central, not ancillary, to student success.
- As educational leaders, they would develop a protocol for changing personal and organizational paradigms for school equity and achievement.
- As educational leaders, they would renew their commitment to the moral purposes of education, which are to make a positive difference in the lives of all citizens and to show individuals how to function together in a society. (Graham & Lindsey, 2002, as cited in Lindsey et al., 2005, p. 81)

This reframing of leadership practice reintroduces a notion that is threaded throughout this book, the notion of a professional practice that starts with us, with an introspective look at our own behaviors, values, and motivations—an "inside-out approach." Since its publication in 1983, Donald Schon's *The Reflective Practitioner: How Professionals Think in Action* has been an important reference for many educators, starting with candidates in teacher education programs right through to expert, experienced practitioners at all levels of the education system. Schon proposed two types of reflection: reflection *on* action and reflection *in* action. Reflection *in action* is defined as the ability of professionals to "think about what they are doing while they are doing it." They may even recognize a new problem(s) and think about it (them) while still acting. This is sometimes called "thinking on our feet." We engage in this type of practice many times every day.

Reflection *on action* is contemplative reflective practice undertaken at a future time to enable us to spend time exploring why we acted as we did, what was happening, how it happened, the feelings and thoughts that were elicited, and so on. In so doing we develop sets of questions and ideas about our activities and practice. Reflective practice is therefore important both for situations that do not go well and those that do go well.

In this book, we offer a variety of opportunities for reflection. Ongoing reflection is an excellent precursor to ongoing assessment. Reflective practice can provide a holistic picture, a "before and after" snapshot that demonstrates strengths and areas for development. We also consider reflective practice to be a critical component for school leaders who are committed to the principles of equity and inclusive education and to whole school/entire school community accountability for school improvement.

We also emphasize the importance of reflecting in concert with others, in order to ensure that we are soliciting multiple perspectives in assessing growth and areas of need. We need others to help us "see" issues and concerns that, for whatever reason, we simply don't see ourselves. In a recent international conference of principals held in Toronto, Roger Martin, dean of The Rotman School of Management, University of Toronto, described the importance of being a leader who engages in "integrative thinking," one who does not simply tolerate or manage diversity of viewpoints, but one who understands the importance of multiple perspectives in a complex and changing world, and who actively seeks them out. The critical consciousness that we have referred to throughout this book, for example, is an invitation to all involved in the school community to engage in assessing the viability of our schools and school communities as equitable and antioppressive spaces, and to share these insights in a safe and open environment.

Here are some additional steps that will be helpful in the monitoring and reporting processes:

1. Planning an Equity Walk: developing expectations for an Equity Walk for staff and administrators

2. Making and recording observations

3. Reflecting and dialoguing with teachers and community members

4. Working with school improvement plans

THE EQUITY WALK

The Equity Walk is a framework to be used for securing account-ability and transparency. It consists of the principal or vice principal walking through the school to assess evidence of an equitable approach to schooling for all students. In certain situations, school administrators may invite or request teachers and/or other school and community members to participate in an Equity Walk. The criteria to be observed are as follows:

- Public space
- Classrooms as learning environments
- Classroom resources
- Purposeful classroom talk (instructional strategies)
- Differentiated instruction
- Differentiated assessment and evaluation
- Parent and community involvement
- Building capacity: professional learning teams
- School improvement plan
- Coinstructional activities
- Additional factors

Each of these criteria is both significant and useful as schools continue to move further toward a culture of evidence-informed decision making. The inclusion of public space, for example, opens up opportunities to gather perceptual and tangible data related to the school's mission, vision, values, beliefs, and attitudes. The way in which public space is defined, maintained, experienced, repro-duced, and transformed has tremendous influence on the social relations of power. What is its significance in the students' and com-munity's negotiation of their identities and their sense of belonging? The messages in the public space are powerful indicators of an equitable school. I remember visiting a kindergarten to Grade 5 school where the entire month's curriculum for each grade was dis-played on the walls in the lobby and updated in a timely fashion.

Everyone in that school knew what was happening and/or what should be happening every day. I immediately felt included and connected. In another school, pictures of multiples of family structures sent a message that all were welcomed and valued.

The information gathered in an Equity Walk is useful in providing support for instructional strategies that lead to student success. In classrooms we look for evidence of differentiation in terms of how student groups are structured, the type of work the students are doing, and how teachers accommodate different learning styles. Active engagement of students promotes equitable outcomes. In an elementary school, all of the components of a balanced or comprehensive literacy plan must be part of the literacy block. The strategies and resources used in the literacy block are an important component of an inclusive classroom. We also look for curriculum approaches, such as the James Banks framework and Mirrors and Windows, that were highlighted in previous chapters. Inclusive programming also ensures that the needs of English language learners and students with special needs are met.

Evidence-Based Decision Making

School teams rely heavily on data collection in developing evidence-based school improvement plans. Data are used to identify and remove barriers to student achievement, to raise awareness about discriminatory practices, and to encourage conversations and collaborative actions about equity issues. Disaggregation of the data allows teams to do a gap analysis and to target specific areas that require improvements. In this way, staff can intentionally effect change for students who are underserved and foster their success. The principal of one secondary school, for example, reports how the staff engaged in collaborative data analysis and determined that "inferencing" was a needed area of focus. They then made use of critical learning pathways to explicitly teach "inferencing," which resulted in improved achievement in reading comprehension. In an Equity Walk, school leaders would also observe collaboration and alignment in content and instructional strategies among teachers in the same subject area and grade as they work in a focus area identified by data analysis.

In Chapter 7 we explored the terrain of parent and community involvement in some depth; however, in terms of an Equity Walk, the principal needs to also closely focus on how parents are involved and what happens as a result of their involvement. What do the parents do differently and what does the teacher do differently in an authentic partnership school? How do the students' interactions and the learning environment change as a result?

School Improvement Planning

Many principals are viewing the walkthrough process as a powerful strategy for improving schools. "The walk-through is a significant step in influencing real change in schools by getting administrators close to the classroom and building their capacity to become instructional leaders" (S. Sather as quoted in Hopkins, 2005/2011). Walkthroughs allow principals and teachers to engage in dialogue and reflection about critical aspects of school improvement—students, curriculum, and achievement. The school improvement planning process is the vehicle for translating collected achievement data into constructive change in the classroom and the school. The Ontario Ministry of Education (2008) reports that a common characteristic of high-performing schools is their practice of translating the planned collection and use of data into priorities, goals, and strategies linked to school improvement planning.

Cocurricular Activities

One of the components for observation on an Equity Walk is the area of coinstructional activities also called cocurricular or extracurricular activities. Epstein (2011) writes as follows:

> Students gain knowledge and build cultural capital when they engage in and enjoy activities, events, and services in school and in their communities. In recent years, after-school programs have become more common, but they do not serve all students at any age or grade level. (p. 380)

Research has revealed the enduring value of visits to museums, zoos, science centers, music and art camps, cultural performances, and talent activities. To remedy the inequities in opportunities for many families, Epstein introduces the idea of an "enrichment voucher"—a kind of "food for thought stamp" that could be subsidized by government or community agencies and distributed to low-income families who wish to develop their children's talents.

The matrix below sets out the above criteria accompanied by a number of activating questions, "look fors" in terms of evidence, and invitations to administrators, staff, parents, and other actors to engage in conversations that promote learning.

Equity Walk in Action

To view an Equity Walk in action, visit the following website: http://www.principals.ca/Display.aspx?cid=8194&pid=8075

The Equity Walk Matrix

The purpose of equity walks is to sharpen and focus the instructional leadership lens and allow the gathering of observational data to confirm or challenge assumptions regarding school improvement and equity in the building(s). Equity walks support ongoing monitoring of implementation. The observational data remains tacit unless there is specific collegial feedback to staff to engage them in reflecting on instruction and assessment.

(Dr. Bev Freedman,
personal correspondence, 2009)

The template for the Equity Walk can be found at the beginning of the Tools and Resources Section at the end of this book. The column headed "To promote learning conversations" would be the area in which you write your comments during your observations; then you can use these notes to dialogue with the teacher about furthering his/her learning or to engage in conversation with those involved to further collective learning.

Tools and Resources

EQUITY WALK MATRIX

The column labeled "To promote learning conversations" would be the area in which you write your comments during your observations and then engage in conversation with those involved to further collective learning.

Equity Component	Question	Evidence You See in School and Classrooms	To promote learning conversations . . .
Public Space	What evidence of equity is demonstrated in the school's public spaces? Is there evidence of inclusion (and inclusive education)? What leadership opportunities are available for students? How do the resource rooms/library demonstrate equity?	• Key messages • Pictures/posters • Significant events/celebrations • Warm and welcoming to parents and community—benches, plants, information • Events supported by the school • Signs in the languages of the community • Family access to the library • Evidence of parent and community volunteers in the school	
Classrooms as Learning Environments	What can you discern from "walking the walls"? How is the learning environment inclusive and reflective of individual learning profiles? What evidence is there of a culture of high expectations?	• Cuing systems • Anchor charts • Exemplars • Rubrics • All students' work represented • Pictures reflect classroom diversity • Seating arrangements	

Equity Component	Question	Evidence You See in School and Classrooms	To promote learning conversations . . .
	What evidence do you see in the environment that demonstrates culturally relevant and responsive teaching and learning? Is the student work visible? Is it some students' work or all students' work? What technology is available for teaching and learning in the classroom environment? Is there evidence of differentiated instruction? Is the learning environment intellectually challenging and stimulating for all learners? How does the learning environment help students develop awareness, understanding, and acceptance of themselves and others?	• Technology: Smart Boards, computers, Elmo presenters, evidence that technology is being actively used	
Classroom Resources	Who is represented and whose voices are heard within the resources? Do the resources promote mastery of broad literacy and numeracy skills? What resources have been provided to support equity (and inclusive education)?	• Resources that are representative of the community and address the differently abled and diverse cultural and racial groups, that are inclusive of different sexual orientations, and that address the needs of recent immigrants, including dual language books	

(Continued)

Equity Component	Question	Evidence You See in School and Classrooms	To promote learning conversations . . .
	Which ones have been provided to support inclusion (and inclusive education)? How are resources used to promote cross-curricular higher level thinking? Are there appropriate resources (computers, Smart Boards, appropriate software) to support students learning with assistive technology? Are resources being used to determine author's message and to develop enduring understanding? How do the resources recognize and value different learning styles?	• Library resources, computers, access to gym, science labs, purposeful timetabling • Targeted resources—assistive and adaptive technology, resources that show appreciation for cultural diversity, resources that show inclusiveness with respect to sensitive issues • Supplementary resources for students who struggle • Leveled books and resources to meet the needs of all learners • Resources reflecting differing interests, learning styles, and multiple intelligences • Support for a variety of languages and cross-curricular themes	
Instructional Core (teacher/ student/ curriculum)	What values and beliefs about equity and inclusive education does the language of the classroom reflect? How are students encouraged to be critical thinkers?	Listen to the language of the classroom • Vocabulary, examples used to illustrate points, critical thinking, and think-alouds—are they scaffolded, and are all students represented? Is the teaching explicit?	

Equity Component	Question	Evidence You See in School and Classrooms	To promote learning conversations . . .
	Is there evidence of students' backgrounds and life experiences being integrated into the lesson?	• Student conversations with one another are respectful	
	What is the ratio of student talk to teacher talk?	• Less teacher talk and more student talk	
	How is oral language supported?	• Extend wait time for students to answer verbal questions: 7 to 10 seconds	
	How is cooperative group learning supported?	• Fewer but more complex questions related to students' experiences	
	Is there evidence of read-alouds, and shared, guided, and independent reading/writing?	• Questions elicit responses using cooperative learning structures as well as responses from individual students	
	What is the explicit evidence of direct connections between intended teaching and intended learning targeting the idea/concept level?	• Students and teachers collaborate on instruction and assessment	
	What evidence is there of students engaged in active dialogue to promote the synthesis and analysis of ideas?	• Evidence of a lot of oral language and cooperative group work	
	Is there an inquiry-based, in-depth approach to teaching?	• All students are represented	
		• Evidence of space to facilitate whole group, small group, pairings, and individual work	

(Continued)

Equity Component	Question	Evidence You See in School and Classrooms	To promote learning conversations . . .
	What evidence is there of teachers being adept at asking higher order thinking questions and encouraging students to think and question?	• Evidence of thoughtful access to computers beyond remedial software and rewards for finishing early	
	Are there uninterrupted scheduled time blocks for learning?	• Feedback is specific and supportive and specifically helps students understand how to improve	
	How does the language of the classrooms reflect the cognitive ability and intellectual curiosity of the students?	• Posted work is used as a cuing system	
	How is technology used as an integrated learning tool?	• Students know both what is being taught and why	
	Is there clear evidence of high expectations for all that enable rich learning related to the curriculum?	Remember	
	How is content being related to broad-based issues, problems, or themes?	• For English language learners (ELLs), it will take three to eight years to reach mastery	
		• Look at student work, desk arrangements, and resources in the classroom and libraries	
Differentiated Instruction	How is differentiated learning being implemented?	• Use of a variety of instructional—whole class, small group, independent—strategies	

Equity Component	Question	Evidence You See in School and Classrooms	To promote learning conversations . . .
	What evidence is there that teaching practice is data informed?	• Use of think-alouds—explicit instruction moving along the continuum at the student's instructional level (as indicated by assessment data) from moderated through shared, guided, and independent strategies	
	How are underachieving students/cohorts being identified?	• Evidence of scaffolding and gradual release of responsibility—from whole class instruction through shared, guided, and independent strategies	
	What evidence is there that individualized education plans/programs (IEPs) are living documents?	• Early and appropriate interventions scaffold learning when students demonstrate limited progress	
	Are gender-specific strategies or interventions used?	• Students' backgrounds are incorporated into the curriculum in terms of choice of resources, examples, and illustrations	
	What instructional strategies are being implemented to meet the needs of students who have additional exceptionalities?	• Students whose language/culture differs from the dominant one have opportunities to develop and consolidate ideas in their own languages—multiliteracies	
	Is there evidence of higher order thinking skills being promoted through the use of teaching strategies that address multiple intelligences?	• Evidence of the use of project-based approaches	
	How is technology being used to address diverse students' needs?		
	How are differentiated opportunities provided for open-ended inquiry and the development of higher level questioning skills?		

(Continued)

(Continued)

Equity Component	Question	Evidence You See in School and Classrooms	To promote learning conversations . . .
		• Evidence of coherent accommodations for students who need them • Purposeful use of modifications to close the achievement gap • Flexible seating arrangements • Flexible learning groups—use student data to group students both heterogeneously and homogeneously • Evidence of purposeful and coherent use of results-based instructional strategies (Marzano, Pickering, & Pollock, 2001; Marzano, Norford, Paynter, Pickering, & Gaddy, 2001) • Use of purposeful nonfiction reading and writing	
Differentiated Assessment & Evaluation	What are the guidelines on assessment and evaluation used in this school/school system? How do you assess if they are fair?	• Formative assessment of students is current and directs the planning for differentiated instruction • Ratio of formative to summative assessments is 65/35. Teachers are	

Equity Component	Question	Evidence You See in School and Classrooms	To promote learning conversations . . .
	What is the student input into assessment and evaluation?	open to a variety of ways for students to demonstrate their learning, e.g., observational, pen and paper, raps, models, graphic organizer	
	Is there evidence of assessment for learning and assessment as learning, and how is this used to drive instruction?	• Students are involved in the design of the assessments and creation of rubrics, anchor charts, and other cuing systems— accountable talk	
	What is the ratio of formative to summative assessment?	• Students develop portfolios and other examples of self-reflective practices to identify personal goals for growth	
	What are the homework policies, and how are they personalized to address diverse learning styles?	• Authentic learning is supported to engage students and meet their needs in learning the skill/concept	
	Is there evidence of students being able to use differing learning styles to complete assignments?	• Students are offered some choice in the product	
	Is a variety of rubrics, anchor charts, exemplars, and checklists evident to enable students to take ownership of their own learning?	• Tracking sheets and tracking boards/e-products are used to record and monitor each student's progress and the collective progress of the class	
	How are rubrics being used for self, peer, and teacher assessment?		

(Continued)

131

Equity Component	Question	Evidence You See in School and Classrooms	To promote learning conversations . . .
	What is the evidence that regular and relevant descriptive feedback is being given to improve student learning? How is moderated marking used to collaboratively assess student work and then to set learning targets?	• Patterns and trends are evident • Student data are used to identify underserved students/cohorts • Student data are used to form cooperative groups • Focused interventions • Involvement in moderated marking	
Parent and Community Involvement	What are the ways parents are informed about their children's learning? Who serves on the school council, and what is the representation from the school, the diverse groups that compose the school population, and the community? What structures are in place to give the community a voice in the development of school goals? Does the school have an action team for partnerships, and if so, how are the actions of parents and community aligned with the school improvement plan?	• Posted messages to parents/caregivers (in different languages for ELLs)—respectful and inclusive • Regular communication home—newsletters, brochures • Inviting website with relevant links to community services • Knowledge of local context—school personnel are knowledgeable about community agencies and access to services parents may need • Surveys assess parents/families on key issues	

Equity Component	Question	Evidence You See in School and Classrooms	To promote learning conversations . . .
	What are the ways parents are both informed about and engaged in their children's development as learners? How are parents and community members welcomed and involved? What partnerships have been formed in the community to support the school and the learner? How has the teacher made use of community resources—human, material, and technological? How do school programs demonstrate responsiveness to the voiced priorities of students, parents, and community? Other than through official reporting periods, how is student progress being communicated to families?	• Involved school council • Engaged action team for partnerships • Welcoming climate that values family and community participation	
Building Capacity: Professional Learning Teams	How is it determined who participates on the learning teams? Does the focus of the teams support equity? In what ways?	• Staff share an in-depth understanding of inclusion and equity and inclusive education and the difference between the two, which is evident in the discussions and work accomplished	

(Continued)

133

(Continued)

Equity Component	Question	Evidence You See in School and Classrooms	To promote learning conversations . . .
	What structures are in place to build and promote collaboration and collective responsibility for equitable learning? Among the teachers, what evidence is there of planning that is strategic, interdisciplinary, (integrated) and targeted? How is student work used by the various learning teams to promote best practices and further equity? What evidence is there of coplanning and coteaching to foster collaboration and better outcomes for learners?	• Professional learning teams use student work and evidence-based high-yield strategies to target closing identified gaps • Staff use resources provided by ministries/departments of education to promote equity and inclusive education—e.g. *Learning for All, Many Roots, Many Voices, Me Read? No Way!, Think Literacy series, Equity and Inclusive Education Strategy,* webinars	
Improvement Plan	What is the involvement of students, parents, and community in the school improvement plan? How do the measurable goals support equity and inclusive education? What process is in use? How are the resources and professional learning aligned to the implementation of the measurable goals?	• Evidence of consultation of partners • Surveys of stakeholders • Teachers share decision making, including goals, targets, resource allocation, and timetable • Students, parents, and staff can articulate the equity priorities of the school—know what they are and why they are in place and feel	

Equity Component	Question	Evidence You See in School and Classrooms	To promote learning conversations . . .
	How is implementation being monitored and assessed? How is staff engaged in review and revision of the school improvement plan?	they are embedded into the school's improvement plan	
Coinstructional Activities	Are all students given opportunities to participate? What are the barriers and enablers? Do the activities reflect students' cultural backgrounds/interests? If socioeconomic status is an issue, what are the compensatory interventions? What is the balance between competitive activities (skill and merit) and inclusive participatory activities (special education)	• Leadership participation is reflective of the student body—student council, grade and school leaders • Team participation is reflective of the student body • There are targeted activities outside of the school day, e.g., breakfast programs, remediation activities	
Additional Factors			

Source: This matrix was developed by Dr. Bev Freedman and adapted by the Ontario Principals' Council Equity and Inclusive Education Team. Reprinted with permission.

Reflective Questions

1. Choose a section of the Equity Walk Matrix and do a "mental walk" through your school. What do you see that supports equity and inclusive education? What is missing? What do you need to check for when you do an actual walk through your school?

2. Who might you include in doing an Equity Walk in your school? Who might "see" things that you might not notice? How might you arrange for flexibility and broad inclusion in this group over time?

3. How might you introduce the use of the Equity Walk Matrix as a tool for assessing and improving equitable practices in your school? What kind of preparation might be needed in your context? What are the steps that you might take to ensure that the Equity Walk is viewed as a catalyst for growth rather than as an evaluative threat?

4. The matrix covers a wide scope. Which aspects (e.g. Public Space, Assessment, Cocurricular Activities) might be easiest or most important to begin with?

5. How might you and your equity team plan to address areas of need that are identified in your equity walkthroughs? How will the results be shared? Are there budgetary, scheduling, professional development, or courageous conversation considerations that you may need to plan for?

Six Levels of Workplace Cultural Proficiency (Workplace and School Settings)

Cultural Destructiveness	Cultural Incapacity	Cultural Blindness	Cultural Precompetence	Cultural Competence	Cultural Proficiency
"See the difference; stomp it out."	*"See the difference; make it wrong."*	*"See the difference; act like you don't."*	*"See the difference; may respond inappropriately or ambiguously."*	*"See the difference; understand the difference that difference makes."*	*"See the difference; respond positively. Engage and adapt."*
Policies, practices, procedures, behaviors attempt to forbid, deny, or limit aspects or displays of one's cultural difference.	**Policies, practices, behaviors that promote the superiority of one culture while excluding, limiting, disrespecting, or disempowering another or other cultures.**	**Policies, practices, behaviors that do not acknowledge differences among/between cultures, and that promote the belief that everyone is served equally by the same policies and practices.**	**New policies, practices, behaviors are developed upon recognizing the limitations of previous knowledge and/or skill to effectively interact with others. Often these new practices are superficial or inappropriate.**	**Policies, practices, behaviors seek to meet the needs of "others" first. Risk-taking behaviors that support equity and fairness are encouraged, modeled, valued, and supported.**	**Esteem difference, ongoing learning about my own and my organization's culture to interact effectively in a variety of cultural groups, now and in the future.**
e.g. • Genocide, exclusion laws/laws denying basic human rights. • Little/no support for differences	e.g. • Expecting "others" to change or "get-over" it. • Blaming others for lack of progress.	e.g. • Discomfort with difference. • Assumed "meritocracy." • Concern about "reverse discrimination."	e.g. • Delegate diversity work to people of color or to a committee. • Quick fix, packaged, short-term programs.	e.g. • Value difference and healthy divergence more than commonality, similarity, and passive compliance. • Assess aspects of culture and how these impact the individual's or	e.g. • Alliance with and advocacy for cultural group who are not majority cultures. • Prefer interdependence

(Continued)

(Continued)

Cultural Destructiveness	Cultural Incapacity	Cultural Blindness	Cultural Precompetence	Cultural Competence	Cultural Proficiency
that impact performance or success. • Avoiding/disallowing certain topics. • Denying time-off for religious observance. • Dress codes prohibit wearing culturally or religiously appropriate garments. • Policy restricting use of one's primary language in the workplace. • Retribution for displaying photo of one's same gender partner in one's office.	• Procedures meet only the needs of the majority culture(s). • Holiday displays promote majority culture, while excluding, limiting, or disrespecting displays of other cultures. • Patterns of recruitment, hiring, and promotion that favor one group over another. • Lowered expectations. • Disproportionate allocation of resources.	• Blindness to the barriers encountered by some cultural groups. • Avoidance of diversity issues is sanctioned and justified by the authority of the manager, majority opinion, or work tasks and schedules. • Belief that agency-sanctioned curriculum benefits all equally.	• Unclear rules, expectations. • Limited accountability for some groups. • Training for staff, not managers. • Multicultural celebrations that promote surface aspects of culture(s).	organization's cross-group effectiveness. • Leverage and manage conflict to learn/grow rather than fear or avoid situations where there are differences of opinions. • Encourage divergence, rather than agreement or consensus, to inform decisions. • Use cultural knowledge to develop the self and organization. Adapt and change as we become aware of our impact/effect on others. • Engage in ongoing learning about the self and others. Behavioral changes become the new standard for behavior and work practices.	rather than independence. • Seek new friends and relationships. • Embrace personal change and transformation. • Seek information from those who are the recipients, audience, or customers of my work in order for my work products and procedures to meet the needs of the OTHER more than MY needs. • Envision and prepare for ever-changing future.

Source: Adapted by Stephanie Graham, Los Angeles County Office of Education, from Lindsey, Nuri Robins, and Terrell (1999). Reprinted with permission.

138

STALKING OUR STORIES, KNOWING OUR SELVES #1

In Search of "Self"	Have you been marginalized?
Unearth	Think back to an incident or situation when you were marginalized by an individual/group/institutionalized situation
Unravel	• On what basis were you marginalized (race, gender, . . .)? How did the event take place? • How did you feel/respond/react? • When did you recognize the oppression (on the spot, much later)?
Understand	• Why did you feel/respond/react in this way? • How were you disempowered? • What were the short- and long-term effects? • What overt or subtle oppression was at play?
Unfold reconsidered attitudes, responses, behaviors	• How would you respond if this were to happen again/continue? • What positions of empowerment might you employ?

STALKING OUR STORIES, KNOWING OUR SELVES #2

In Search of "Self"	Have you or your school marginalized others?
Unearth	Think of a situation when you or your school were involved in marginalizing another person or group.
Unravel	On what basis did you, either intentionally or inadvertently, marginalize another person/group? How did you think/act inappropriately? When did you recognize/become aware of the oppression? What do you think the effects (short- and long-term) might have been on others?
Understand	Why might you have acted in this way (lack of knowledge, background experience, acculturation/ normalization . . .)
Unfold reconsidered attitudes, responses, and behaviors	How have/might your attitudes and responses change? What different actions would be appropriate?

BUILDING A CULTURAL PROFILE

The dominant group within each subculture is bolded in each category.

Components of Cultural Identity	My Location, Relationships, and Experiences	Influences on My Identity as a Person and as an Educator
Class Below poverty line, homeless, working class, lower middle class **Middle class, upper class**		
Gender/Gender Orientation **Male** Female **Heterosexual** Homosexual Bisexual Transgender		
Race American Indian/First Nation, Métis, Inuit **White** Black Asian Other		
Ethnicity **Western European** Central/Eastern European Latino Asian African Caribbean Other		

Components of Cultural Identity	My Location, Relationships, and Experiences	Influences on My Identity as a Person and as an Educator
Age Child Youth **Young adult** **Middle aged** Senior		
Language **English** Bilingual (including English) English as a Second Language Multilingual Non-English speaking		
Religion **Christian (Protestant)** Christian (Catholic) Christian (other, e.g., Mormon) Jewish, Islamic, Hindu, Buddhist Other		
Physical Context Urban, suburban, rural Geographic region Environment (coastal, mountains, prairies, desert)		

LADDER OF INFERENCE

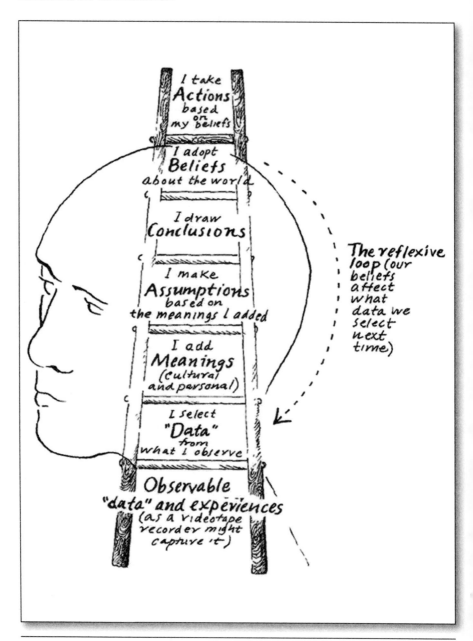

Source: Ladder of Inference, by Chris Argyris, as shown in Senge, Kleiner, Roberts, Ross, and Smith (1994).

JAMES A. BANKS'S INCLUSIVE CURRICULUM FRAMEWORK

Model / Level	The Roles of the Student and Teacher	The School's Relationship to Its Community
Level 1 The Contributions Approach	Adding diverse heroes and heroines, holidays and celebrations to the curriculum selected using criteria similar to those used to select mainstream heroes and heroines for the existing curriculum *Role of Student:* Passive recipient of information *Role of Teacher:* Provider of all information; structures materials, use of resources, and time allocation	Not engaged
Level 2 The Additive Approach	Adding a variety of content, concepts, themes, and perspectives to the existing curriculum without changing its basic structure *Role of Student:* Passive recipient of information *Role of Teacher:* Provider of all information; structures materials, use of resources, and time allocation	Some acquaintance with school communities as sources of information
Level 3 The Transformation Approach	Changing the actual structure of the curriculum to enable students to view concepts, issues, events, and themes from the perspectives of diverse groups *Role of Student:* Active learner *Role of Teacher:* Facilitator of learning opportunities for students to explore multiple perspectives, major concepts, big ideas, and general principles and to apply ideals such as fairness, equity, or justice to their world	Growing partnership
Level 4 The Social Action Approach	Allowing students to make decisions on important social issues and take actions to help solve them *Role of Student:* Active/activist learner *Role of Teacher:* Facilitator of learning opportunities for students to explore multiple perspectives, major concepts, big ideas, and general principles and to apply ideals such as fairness, equity, or justice to their world.	Engaged partnership

Source: Adapted from *James Banks Model*, by Toronto District School Board, n.d., http://www.tdsb.on.ca/_site/viewitem.asp?siteid=15&menuid=8797&pageid=7697. Adapted with permission.

ACKNOWLEDGING POWER WHEEL

Who Am I?

1. Socioeconomic background
2. Ethnic background
3. Race/color
4. Language background
5. Religious background
6. Geographic origin
7. Education
8. Gender
9. Sexual orientation
10. Age
11. Physical/mental ability
12. Other

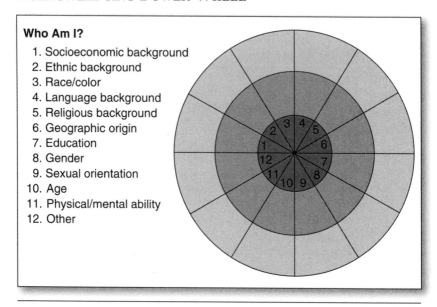

Source: Adapted from Lee (1992, p. 11).

References

Achbar, M. (Ed.). (1994). *Manufacturing consent: Noam Chomsky and the media.* Montreal, QC: Black Rose Books.

Armstrong, D. E., & McMahon, B. J. (2006). *Inclusion in urban educational environments: Addressing issues of diversity, equity, and social justice.* Charlotte, NC: Information Age.

Banks, J. A. (1994). Transforming the mainstream curriculum. *Educational Leadership, 51*(8), 4–8.

Bell, L. A. (2008). Expanding definitions of good teaching. In M. Pollock (Ed.), *Everyday antiracism: Getting real about race in school* (pp. 287–290). New York, NY: The New Press.

Bigelow, B., & Peterson, B. (Eds.). (1998). *Rethinking Columbus: The next 500 years.* (2nd ed.). Milwaukee, WI: Rethinking Schools.

Blum, R. W., McNeely, C. A., & Rinehart, P. M. (2002). *Improving the odds: The untapped power of schools to improve the health of teens.* Minneapolis, MN: Center for Adolescent Health, University of Minnesota.

Brant, B. (1994). *Writing as witness: Essay and talk.* Toronto, ON: Women's Press.

Briskin, L. (2001). Power in the classroom. In J. Newton (Ed.), *Voices from the classroom: Reflections on teaching and learning in higher education* (pp. 25–39). Toronto, ON: Broadview Press.

Brookover, W. B., & Lezotte, L. W. (1979). *Changes in school characteristics coincident with changes in student achievement* (Occasional Paper No. 17). East Lansing: Michigan State University, East Lansing Institute for Research in Teaching.

CampbellJones, B. (2008). *Norms of operation.* In F. CampbellJones & B. CampbellJones (Facilitators), *Symposium on human rights, antiracism and cultural proficiency.* Symposium conducted by Ontario Principals' Council Education Leadership Canada, Toronto, ON.

CampbellJones, B., CampbellJones, F., & Lindsey, R. (2010). *The cultural proficiency journey: Moving beyond ethical barriers toward profound school change.* Thousand Oaks, CA: Corwin.

Center for Social and Emotional Education. (2009). *School climate research summary.* New York, NY: Author.

Chabris, C., & Simons, D. (2010). *The invisible gorilla: How our intuitions deceive us.* New York, NY: Crown.

Clandinin, D. J., & Connelly, F. M. (2000). *Narrative inquiry: Experience and story in qualitative research.* San Francisco, CA: Jossey-Bass.

Cohen, J., Pickeral, T., & McCloskey, M. (2008/2009). The challenge of assessing school climate. *Educational Leadership, 66*(4). Retrieved from http://www.ascd.org/publications/educational_leadership/dec08/vol66/num04/The_Challenge_of_Assessing_School_Climate.aspx

Craig, W. M., & Pepler, D. J. (1998). Observations of bullying and victimization in the school yard. *Canadian Journal of School Psychology, 13*(2), 41–59.

Cross, T. L., Bazron, B. J., Dennis, K. W., & Isaacs, M. R. (1989). *Toward a culturally competent system of care: A monograph on effective services for minority children who are severely emotionally disturbed.* Washington, DC: CASSP Technical Assistance Center, Georgetown University Child Development Center.

Crozier, L. (host). (2011). *We are the 10%.* [Radio program]. In P. Bertrand (Executive producer), *The Current.* Toronto, ON: CBC Radio-Canada.

Dei, G. J. S. (2003). Communicating across the tracks: Challenges for anti-racist educators in Ontario today. *Orbit, 33*(3), 1–5.

Dei, G. J. S. (2006, September 28). *Meeting equity fair and square.* Keynote address to the Leadership Conference of the Elementary Teachers' Federation of Ontario, Mississauga, ON.

Delhi, K. (1995). What's love got to do with it? The Commission's approach to community education. *Orbit, 26*(2), pp. 19–23.

Delisio, E. R. (2006). Improving school culture. *Education World, 24*(5), 161–173.

Delpit, L. (1988). The silenced dialogue: Power and pedagogy in educating other people's children. *Harvard Educational Review, 58*(3), 280–298.

Delpit, L. (1995). *Other people's children: Cultural conflict in the classroom.* New York, NY: The New Press.

DuFour, R., DuFour, R., Eaker, R., & Karhanek, G. (2004). *Whatever it takes: How professional learning communities respond when kids don't learn.* Bloomington, IN: Solution Tree.

Edmonds, R. (1979). Effective schools for the urban poor. *Educational Leadership, 37*(1), 15–24.

Epstein, J. L. (2011). *School, family, and community partnerships: Preparing educators and improving schools* (2nd ed.). Boulder, CO: Westview Press.

Epstein, J. L. (n.d.). *Center on school, family, and community partnerships* [Website introduction]. Retrieved from http://www.csos.jhu.edu/p2000/center.htm

Epstein, J. L., et al. (2002). *School, family, and community partnerships: Your handbook for action* (2nd ed.). Thousand Oaks, CA: Corwin.

Forced choice. (2011). *Teampedia: Tools for teams.* Retrieved from http://www.teampedia.net/wiki/index.php?title=Forced_Choice

General Assembly of the United Nations. (1989/1990). *Convention on the rights of the child.* Retrieved from http://www.crin.org/docs/resources/treaties/uncrc.asp

Gilroy, P. (1991). *There ain't no black in the Union Jack.* Chicago, IL: University of Chicago Press.

Goleman, D. (1985). *Vital lies, simple truths: The psychology of self-deception.* New York: Simon & Schuster.

Greenfield, T. B., & Ribbins, P. (Eds.). (1993). *Greenfield on educational administration: Towards a humane science.* New York, NY: Routledge.

Haberman, M. (1991). The pedagogy of poverty versus good teaching. *Phi Delta Kappan, 73,* 290–294.

Hall, S. (2006). Cultural identity and diaspora. In J. E. Braziel & A. Mannur (Eds.), *Theorizing diaspora* (pp. 233–246). Malden, MA: Blackwell.

Hamann, E. T. (2008). Standards vs. 'standard' knowledge. In M. Pollock (Ed.). *Everyday antiracism: Getting real about race in school* (pp. 98–101). New York, NY: The New Press.

Hannum, K. (2007*). Social identity: Knowing yourself, leading others.* Greensboro, NC: Center for Creative Leadership.

Henderson, A. T., Mapp, K. L., Johnson, V. R., & Davies, D. (2007). *Beyond the bake sale: The essential guide to family-school partnerships.* New York, NY: The New Press.

Hilliard, A. G., III. (1989). Teachers and cultural styles in a pluralistic society. *NEA Today, 7*(6), 65–69.

Hilliard, A. G., III, & Sizemore, B. (1984). *Saving the African American child: A report of the Task Force on Black Academic and Cultural Excellence.* Washington, DC: National Alliance of Black School Educators.

hooks, b. (1990). *Yearning: Race, gender, and cultural politics.* Boston, MA: South End Press.

Hopkins, G. (2005/2011). Walk-throughs are on the move. *Education World.* Retrieved from http://www.educationworld.com/a_admin/admin/admin405.shtml

Institute for Education Leadership. (2008). *Putting Ontario's leadership framework into action: A guide for school and system leaders.* Toronto, ON: Author.

Kose, B. W. (2009). The principal's role in professional development for social justice: An empirically-based transformative framework. *Urban Education, 44,* 628–663.

Ladd, H. F., & Zelli, A. (2002). School-based accountability in North Carolina: The responses of school principals. *Educational Administration Quarterly, 38*(4), 494–529.

Lee, E. (1992). *Letters to Marcia: A teacher's guide to anti-racist education*. Toronto, ON: Centre for Cross Cultural Communication.

Lezotte, L. (1997). *Learning for all*. Okemo, MI: Effective Schools Products.

Lindsey, R. B., Nuri Robins, K., & Terrell, R. D. (1999). *Cultural proficiency: A manual for school leaders*. Thousand Oaks, CA: Corwin.

Lindsey, R. B., Nuri Robins, K., & Terrell, R. D. (2003). *Cultural proficiency: A manual for school leaders* (2nd ed.). Thousand Oaks, CA: Corwin.

Lindsey, R. B., Roberts, L. M., & CampbellJones, F. (2005) *The culturally proficient school: An implementation guide for school leaders*. Thousand Oaks, CA: Corwin.

MacNeil, A., & Maclin, V. (2005, July 24). Building a learning community: The culture and climate of schools. Retrieved from the *Connexions* website: http://cnx.org/content/m12922/1.2

Marzano, R. J., Norford, J. S., Paynter, D. J., Pickering, D. J., & Gaddy, B. B. (2001). *Handbook for classroom instruction that works*. Alexandria, VA: ASCD.

Marzano, R. J., Pickering, D. J., & Pollock, J. E. (2001). *Classroom instruction that works: Research-based strategies for increasing student achievement*. Alexandria, VA: ASCD.

McCarthy, C. (1993). After the canon: Knowledge and ideological representation in the multicultural discourse on curriculum reform. In C. McCarthy & W. Crichlow (Eds.), *Race, identity, and representation in education* (pp. 289–305). New York, NY, & London, England: Routledge.

McIntosh, P. (1988). *White privilege: The invisible knapsack*. Wellesley, MA: Wellesley College Center for Research on Women.

McKenzie, K., Christman, D., Hernandez, F., Fierro, E., Capper, C., Dantley, M., Gonzalez, M., et al. (2008). Educating leaders for social justice: A design for a comprehensive, social justice leadership preparation program. *Educational Administration Quarterly, 44*(1), 111–138.

McMurtry, R., & Curling, A. (2008). *The review of the roots of youth violence* (Vol. 2: Executive summary). Toronto: Queen's Printer for Ontario.

National Commission on Excellence in Education. (1983). *A nation at risk*. Washington, DC: U.S. Department of Education.

Ontario Ministry of Education. (2008). *Using data to improve student achievement*. Toronto, ON: Author. Retrieved from http://www.edu.gov.on.ca/eng/literacynumeracy/inspire/research/Using_Data.pdf

Ontario Ministry of Education. (2009a). *Equity and inclusive education in Ontario schools: Guidelines for policy development and implementation*. Toronto: Author.

Ontario Ministry of Education. (2009b). *Realizing the promise of diversity: Ontario's equity and inclusive education strategy*. Toronto, ON: Author.

Ontario Ministry of Education. (2010). *Parents in partnership: A parent engagement policy for Ontario schools.* Toronto, ON: Author.

Ontario Principals' Council. (2010). Videos & reflective questions. [Equity and inclusive leadership web modules]. Retrieved from http://www.principals.ca/Display.aspx?cid=8194&pid=8075

Module 1—Leading Expert Voices from the Field
Module 2—Critical Issues in Equity and Inclusive Education: Part 1
Module 3—Critical Issues in Equity and Inclusive Education: Part 2
Module 4—Equity Frameworks
Module 5—Leading the Inclusive School, Part 1
Module 6—Leading the Inclusive School: Part 2
Module 7—Closing the Achievement Gap
Module 8—Engaging Parents and Communities
Module 9—Equity Walk: A Research-Informed Equity Practice

Ontario Safe Schools Action Team. (2005). *Shaping safer schools: A bullying prevention action plan.* Toronto, ON: Author.

Pollock, M. (2008). *Everyday antiracism: Getting real about race in school.* New York, NY: The New Press.

Portelli, J., Shields, C., & Vibert, A. (2007). *Toward an equitable education: Poverty, diversity, and students at risk—The National Report.* Toronto: Ontario Institute for Studies in Education.

Preble, B., & Taylor, L. (2008/2009). School climate through students' eyes. *Educational Leadership, 66*(4), 35–40.

Pushor, D., & Ruitenberg, C. (2005). *Parent engagement and leadership.* Saskatoon, SK: Dr. Stirling McDowell Foundation for Research Into Teaching.

Reese, R. (2001). Building cultural bridges in schools: The colorful flags model. *Journal of Race, Ethnicity, and Education, 4*(3), 277–304. Retrieved from http://www.csupomona.edu/~rrreese/BRIDGING.HTML

Reeves, D. (2006). *The learning leader: How to focus school improvement for better results.* Alexandria, VA: ASCD.

Ryan, J. (2003). *Leading diverse schools.* Dordrecht, The Netherlands: Kluwer Academic.

Ryan, J. (2006). *Inclusive leadership.* San Francisco, CA: Jossey-Bass.

Sanders, M. G., & Sheldon, S. B. (2009). *Principals matter: A guide to school, family, and community partnerships.* Thousand Oaks, CA: Corwin.

Schargel, R. P., Thacker, T., & Bell, J. (2007). *From at-risk to academic excellence: What successful leaders do.* Larchmont, NY: Eye on Education.

Schon, D. (1983). *The reflective practitioner: How professionals think in action.* New York: Basic Books.

Senge, P. M., Kleiner, A., Roberts, C., Ross, R., & Smith, B. (1994). *The fifth discipline fieldbook: Strategies and tools for building a learning organization.* New York, NY: Currency Doubleday.

Shields, C. M. (2005). What is a good school? In W. Hare & J. P. Portelli (Eds.), *Key questions for educators* (pp. 77–80). Halifax, NS: Edphil Books.

Singleton, G. E., & Hays, C. (2008). Beginning courageous conversations about race. In M. Pollock (Ed.), *Everyday antiracism: Getting real about race in school* (pp. 18–23). New York, NY: The New Press.

Sizer, T. R. (1984). *Horace's compromise: The dilemma of the American high school.* Boston, MA: Houghton Mifflin.

Sizer, T. R. (1992). *Horace's school: Redesigning the American high school.* Boston: Houghton Mifflin.

Sizer, T. R. (1996). *Horace's hope: What works for the American high school.* Boston, MA: Houghton Mifflin.

Sleeter, C. (2008). Involving students in selecting reading materials. In M. Pollock (Ed.), *Everyday antiracism: Getting real about race in school* (pp. 150–152). New York, NY: The New Press.

Sleeter, C. (2011). Interviewed by A. Mishra. *Politics of justice more than a politics of recognition.* Retrieved from http://deshkaledu.org/Interviews .htm

Solomon, P. (2002). School leaders and anti-racism: Overcoming pedagogical and political obstacles. *Journal of School Leadership, 12,* 174–197.

Style, E. (1996). *Curriculum as window and mirror.* Wellesley, MA: Wellesley College Center for Research on Women. Retrieved from http://www.wcwonline.org/Projects-Extra-Information/seed-curriculum-as-window-a-mirror

Terrell, R. D., & Lindsey, R. B. (2009). *Culturally proficient leadership: The personal journey begins within.* Thousand Oaks, CA: Corwin.

Theoharis, G. (2007). Social justice educational leaders and resistance: Toward a theory of social justice leadership. *Educational Administration Quarterly, 43*(2), 221–258.

Tomlinson, (2000). Presidential address: Power and privilege in education: The perpetual problem of social class. *Irish Educational Studies, 19*(1), 1–15.

Toronto District School Board. (2005). *Stop the world: I want to get on.* Retrieved from http://tdsbstreamvip.tdsb.on.ca/tdsb/Equity/Stop_The_World_I_Want_To_Get_On.wmv

Toronto District School Board. (2006). *Equitable schools: Gender equity resource guide.* Toronto, ON: Author. Retrieved from http://www.tdsb .on.ca/wwwdocuments/programs/Equity_in_Education/docs/PS03160% 20Gender%20Equity%20Resource%20Guide%20.pdf

Toronto District School Board. (n.d.) *James Banks model.* Retrieved from http://www.tdsb.on.ca/_site/viewitem.asp?siteid=15&menuid=8797& pageid=7697

Vinson, K., Gibson, R., & Ross, E. W. (2001). High-stakes testing and standardization: The threat to authenticity. *Monograph in Progressive Perspectives*. University of Vermont: John Dewey Project on Progressive Education.

Worthy, J. (2008, October). Panel speaker. In F. CampbellJones & B. CampbellJones (Facilitators), *Symposium on human rights, antiracism and cultural proficiency*. Symposium conducted by Ontario Principals' Council Education Leadership Canada, Toronto, ON.

Yon, D. (1995). Identity and difference in the Caribbean diaspora: Case study from metropolitan Toronto. In A. Ruprecht & C. Taiana (Eds.), *The reordering of culture: Latin America, the Caribbean and Canada* (pp. 479–498). Ottawa, ON: Carleton University Press.

Zoric, T., Charania, G. R., & Jeffers, K. (2003). School groups and clubs: Promoting equity minded student leadership. *Orbit, 33*(3), 26–28.

Index

CORWIN

A SAGE Company

The Corwin logo—a raven striding across an open book—represents the union of courage and learning. Corwin is committed to improving education for all learners by publishing books and other professional development resources for those serving the field of PreK–12 education. By providing practical, hands-on materials, Corwin continues to carry out the promise of its motto: **"Helping Educators Do Their Work Better."**